Managing Supplier-Related Processes

Other Paton Professional books by Denise Robitaille:

The (Almost) Painless ISO 9001:2000 Transition
Corrective Action for the Software Industry (with Johanna Rothman)
The Corrective Action Handbook
Document Control
The Management Review Handbook
The Preventive Action Handbook
Root Cause Analysis

Managing Supplier-Related Processes

Denise Robitaille

PROFESSIONAL

Paton Professional
Chico, California

Most Paton Professional books are available at quantity discounts when purchased in bulk. For more information, contact:

Paton Professional
A division of Paton Press LLC
P.O. Box 44
Chico, CA 95927-0044
Telephone: (530) 342-5480
Fax: (530) 342-5471
E-mail: *books@patonprofessional.com*
Web: *www.patonprofessional.com*

11 10 09 08 07   5 4 3 2 1

ISBN-13: 1-978-1-932828-14-6
ISBN-10: 1-932828-14-1

Library of Congress Cataloging-in-Publication Data
Robitaille, Denise E.
Managing supplier-related processes / by Denise Robitaille.
p. cm.
Includes index.
ISBN 978-1-932828-14-6
1. Industrial procurement. 2. Purchasing departments. 3. Purchasing—Management. I. Title.
HD39.5.R63 2007
658.7'2—DC22

2007010731

Staff
Publisher: Scott M. Paton
Editor: Karen Bleske
Book design: David Hurst
Cover: Caylen Balmain

Contents

Introduction

"For the want of a nail, the shoe was lost; for the want of a shoe, the horse was lost; and for the want of a horse, the rider was lost, being overtaken and slain by the enemy, all for the want of care about a horseshoe nail."
—Benjamin Franklin

This book is about addressing those "wants" that can have a profound effect on our ability to serve our customers. Recognizing which products and services are most critical to the health of any organization is an essential task. The outcome will vary because all of us have different clients and markets, and, therefore, we need different resources, materials, and services to satisfy our customers. This book is intended to help bring definition, consistency, and effectiveness to the process of managing the relationship with the organizations that fulfill this important role in our quality management systems—the suppliers.

Chapter 1

Your Suppliers

Without suppliers, we're all out of business. It doesn't matter what kind of business we're in. At one time or another—usually daily—we rely on our suppliers for goods and services that make it possible for us to fulfill our customers' requirements.

Suppliers are an essential constituent of commerce. They represent the myriad organizations that produce the raw materials, tools, machinery, components, software, telecommunications, literature, packaging, and transportation you need to get your product to market. Any part, function, or service that doesn't originate within the boundaries you define as your organization is the product of a supplier.

You could have the finest design, the best-qualified staff, and the most efficient processes, but if you can't get quality raw material on time at a reasonable price, your designs will be relegated to the drawing board and production equipment will remain idle. Service industries and nonprofit organizations are equally vulnerable. None of us can claim to have complete autonomy. We all have some level of dependency on suppliers.

Conversely, without your company (and others like yours), suppliers wouldn't have customers. You create their market. Therefore, your relationship with your vendors is symbiotic. You rely on one another for your viability; you're dependent on one another for your very survival.

ISO 9004 enumerates eight quality management principles that are the hallmarks of successful organizations. These principles underlie the policies and practices characterizing a well-developed quality management system (QMS). Eighth on the list of these management principles is "mutually beneficial supplier relationships." It states: "An organization and its suppliers are interdependent and a mutually beneficial relationship enhances the ability of both to create value." This principle lays the foundation for the ISO 9001 requirements dealing with purchasing and supplier relations.

Regardless of the QMS model used or the nature of the industry, it's essential for an organization to acknowledge the role that suppliers play in the fulfillment of its goals. Suppliers are one of a group of stakeholders who are external to your organization. Even if they're halfway around the globe, their stake in your success makes them a virtual extension of your business. They have enormous influence on the effectiveness of your QMS—which translates into your ability to serve your customers.

Similarly, the nature of your own company's interaction with them will directly affect their organizations and influence their ability to serve all their customers—not just you. That influence can be either positive or negative. For example, your mandates for price reductions will probably cause them to expend resources investigating lower-priced components or developing more efficient processes. This could manifest itself in several ways. Your suppliers may:

■ Develop more streamlined practices to address overhead costs, such as lowering minimum inventory levels or relaxing incoming inspection criteria

■ Find more competitively priced components from alternate vendors

■ Buy cheaper parts and hope they don't affect product quality

■ Reduce their profit margins and pray they make up the difference in volume

■ Say "No," leaving you with one fewer qualified supplier and stuck trying to find a good replacement.

You may be the direct cause of their developing a more efficient and "leaner" approach to a process. Or you may put them out of business by making repeated unreasonable demands. It's worth repeating: Good supplier relations should enhance value for both parties.

It's sobering to contemplate that we sometimes convey the same outrageous ultimatums to our suppliers as the ones we grudgingly receive from our customers.

When organizations get requests from their customers for lower prices, they often pass the ultimatum on to their own suppliers. Although that isn't necessarily inappropriate, it shouldn't be the first or only course of action. The troublesome mind-set this tactic reflects is the (often unsupported) opinion that the vendor is always holding back or making obscene profits at its customers' expense. The question to ask is whether you are receiving goods and services at a fair price. Are you getting the requisite bang for your buck? If the answer is yes, then you must consider the possibility that a request for price concessions may not be the best course of action for you or your supplier.

Everyone needs to make a profit. If your suppliers aren't making money they won't be in business very long. And then where will you go to get your raw materials? Will the expenses incurred in researching alternate sources, conducting qualification audits, getting parts approvals, forging relationships with new technical support personnel, and so forth outweigh the cost of staying with a reliable and established vendor?

Good supplier relations have advantages, such as the transfer of knowledge and the benchmarking of excellent practices that benefit both organizations. For example, the sharing of information may net a significant decrease in the number of defects a vendor is experiencing because of an out-of-control process. Your input can help the vendor reduce costs and enable it to get good product to you faster and more reliably. The influence organizations exercise over the quality of the products their suppliers furnish them can be profound.

THE SUPPLY CHAIN

An organization is usually and concurrently the customer of one entity and the supplier to another in a (sometimes) lengthy chain. Process approach transcends organizational barriers as the output of one company becomes the input for its customer. When there's a problem with one supplier, the effect is felt all along the chain.

The cascading effect of falling dominoes becomes an appropriate analogy. Consider: A supplier of stainless steel bar stock is one week late making a delivery to a manufacturer of precision fasteners. The fastener manufacturer is late getting the shipment out to the company that makes electronic connectors. The supplier of the connectors misses the delivery date to the assembly house that fabricates wire harnesses. The wire harnesses arrive at the robotic manufacturer two weeks late. It misses its delivery to its customer by almost one month. (The ultimate irony would be if the robotic device were installed in a piece of machinery that speeded up loading raw material—such as stainless steel—for shipment.) Variations on this scenario play themselves out on the global stage every day.

The challenge of remaining competitive, effective, and responsive in a volatile marketplace is something all companies have in common. Even nonprofit organizations aren't immune to this challenge as they compete for limited funds and toil to balance their budgets and contain their expenses so that they can continue to serve their clients.

Organizations struggle with balancing the need to have resources readily available from suppliers against the need to minimize their own inventories. Their suppliers, facing comparable constraints, react similarly, sometimes imperiling their ability to serve their customers. Everyone is committed to remaining lean, often targeting inventory as an overhead cost to be reduced in the pursuit of competitiveness and increased revenues. Unfortunately, organizations may not give appropriate weight to the analysis of factors such as established lead times, customer orders, history, and projections. They ignore these objective inputs into the decision-making process that should drive their production schedule because they've been given a mandate to keep inventory levels low. Like just about everything else, the appropriateness of this strategy should be subject to scrutiny. What's the risk? What will ultimately cost more? Are you willing to risk a late delivery to get a lower price? Have you investigated the hidden cost of express shipments? Or is the criticality of on-time delivery so great that you're willing to pay a little more to do business with a supplier that has a guaranteed inventory?

Organizations must weigh multiple constraints against mandated requirements. Having comprehensive knowledge of capacity, constraints, engineering forte, and the market enables an organization to define itself in relation to its customers and its competition. This helps it develop its targeted customer base. For example, some seek to establish niche markets; others make their reputations on fastest turnaround. Large mass producers and small specialty shops all have their places. This same information drives the selection of the suppliers that will best suit your needs. Do you know your suppliers' forte? You must look not only at the product but also at the capacity of the supplier's management system to consistently fulfill your requirements. Those may relate to delivery, traceability, responsiveness to change, compliance with regulatory constraints, conformance to sector-specific certification schemes, familiarity with your market, and so forth.

Customer satisfaction means delivering the product in accordance with customer requirements. Some customers eschew pricing concerns in exchange for same-day delivery. Others don't need (or want) the most sophisticated high-end components because they are being installed in devices with very short life cycles. You don't need a two-year battery for a device that will last only three months.

All of these factors play a part in decisions companies make about the products they sell. Therefore, it's important to define what you need from a vendor. You must establish how you will go about selecting and evaluating suppliers to determine if they can fulfill your requirements.

DEFINING YOUR REQUIREMENTS

The extent to which you can satisfy your customer directly depends upon the effectiveness of your process for procuring goods and services. As with all other processes in your QMS, the manner in which you manage supplier-related processes must reflect the needs of your organization. What matters to a chemical plant is not applicable to a software developer. Call centers will care about their telecommunications provider; rapid-delivery services will care about the vendor to whom they subcontract their vehicle maintenance. The same commodity can have different levels of importance depending on the organization. Whereas shipping hazardous products requires corrugated boxes and special packaging that has to meet strict international regulations, other items simply require a container that will hold a lightweight, nonflammable, unbreakable object.

Criteria, classification, authorizations, controls, documents, and records are all features of this process that you must define. Companies often fail to give adequate attention to identifying their requirements. What do we require of our vendors? How will we select the best suppliers for our organization? What methods will we use to evaluate and qualify them? Will there be different criteria for different commodities or classifications? Is there more than one process? Who is authorized to qualify a vendor? How, and to whom, do we communicate vendor status? What techniques will we use to measure their success in meeting our requirements? How will we know if a vendor's capacity to serve our needs changes through time? How do we handle risk?

Answering these kinds of questions will drive the implementation of a supplier-qualification program that will add value to your organization. It will facilitate the integration of the supplier and its products into your QMS so that you can achieve optimum value from the relationship.

Suppliers come in all shapes and sizes. Depending on the nature of your organization, the following is a sampling of the diverse companies that might be represented on your approved vendor list:

- Distributors of generic parts
- "Temp" agencies
- Associations that publish industry standards
- Chemicals manufacturers
- Sheet metal shops
- Foundries

■ Utility companies
■ Other divisions or subsidiaries of your own company
■ Contract assembly houses.

At first glance, they seem to be a hodgepodge of unrelated items thrown together. The one common denominator is that they are all examples of purveyors of goods and services essential to your QMS.

They all have a role to play in your supply chain. Some will interact with your organization only through their Web sites. You will speak to others regularly to place standard purchase orders. You will contract with some firms for one project and some companies will sell you one piece of capital equipment. You may establish long-term partnerships with others. Defining how these relationships fit into your QMS will bring consistency and control to the processes and functions with which they are associated.

This book addresses the challenge of achieving good supplier relations. Deciding with whom to do business, establishing criteria that reflect your needs, and developing a monitoring system that provides you the information you need to assess the performance of your suppliers are all aspects of managing your supply chain. This book will present tools and techniques to ease the process and create value for your organization. It covers:

■ The purchasing function
■ Outsourced processes
■ Classification and categorization
■ Supplier qualification
■ Monitoring
■ Supplier corrective actions
■ Relationship to the management review process.

This list includes consideration of the features of all well-controlled processes: definition, resource allocation, planning, implementation, interaction with related processes, measurement, verification, and continual improvement.

Chapter 2

Purchasing Department Versus Purchasing Process

I t's not unreasonable to expect that the purchasing process would fall under the purview of the purchasing department. It's logical. However, the reality is that in most organizations people from many different departments generate purchase orders and sign contracts. Not all procurement is done by the purchasing department.

The prevailing tendency in many organizations continues to be to associate a process predominantly (if not exclusively) with one particular department or area of the organization. This perpetuates what has been referred to as the "silo" approach to defining the organization, in which each activity is treated as a unique self-contained unit that has little interaction beyond its scope. In this case, it means that the purchasing department owns the process for procurement of goods and services. Consequently, the purchasing procedure describes what the purchasing department does. Similarly, the contract review procedure (a term left over from ISO 9001:1994) continues to describe what happens in the customer service department. In both cases, this practice ignores the reality that people in multiple departments take orders from customers or place orders with vendors. Even if they don't place orders, they may request quotes, discuss engineering changes, revise deliveries, or process any number of contract amendments. In smaller organizations it's not uncommon for salespeople to expedite purchase orders to help their customers and for purchasing or engineering people to speak with customers about changes that may affect product or delivery. There is no right or wrong to these practices. It's how companies operate.

The process approach to systems management requires that you consider the process: First, within the context of organizational inputs and outputs; second, as it relates to the area in which it occurs, for the purpose of definition, authorization, and control. So you must begin by looking at the input that has generated the requirement to buy a product or service. In a manufacturing environment, the trigger (input) is the processing of a customer's order. You need to buy raw material, tooling, and components to manufacture the product. The sequence and flow is clear and direct.

In a medical lab, the requirements might involve the purchase of disposable supplies such as gloves and masks; in a software company, the process might begin with the acquisition of appropriate software or the hiring of contract personnel, such as programmers and test engineers. The process flow doesn't always follow a direct path back to the purchasing department. In these examples, the lab personnel could be authorized to buy their own supplies. In the software company, the human resource department could be the function that approves outside contractors and consultants.

This is important because the purchasing process is one of the features of your organization that permeates the entire quality management system (QMS) with resulting interfaces in myriad departments and functions. It's the process for controlling the acquisition and delivery of the resources required to carry out other processes. In addition to the raw materials needed for manufacturing, you need a whole bunch of other "stuff" to bring your product to market. The quality control (QC) lab authorizes the local metrology house to come in and calibrate equipment. The human resource department contracts with the temp agency for seasonal workers. The production manager initials the shop order for the purchase of repair parts for equipment. The shipping department signs off on the requisition that accompanies parts that are sent out for plating. The examples go on and on.

The process approach gives us the mandate and the flexibility to identify other related processes and functions in which purchasing might occur. Nothing is wrong with having people other than the purchasing agent signing orders for goods and services. We must get beyond the classic paradigm of purchasing agents' buying raw material and components and address how we typically acquire all this other "stuff" we need to run the business and keep customers happy.

Organizations must establish procedures and protocols that work best for them. QMS models, such as ISO 9001, require you to:

- Define the process.
- Say who is authorized.
- Ensure that the practice is implemented and adequately controlled.

A KNOWLEDGE GAP

Purchases of raw materials, components, and tooling are generally routed through the company's purchasing department. Purchasing procedures usually provide extensive details of what the purchasing department does. Unfortunately, there is rarely sufficient language in the typical documentation to define alternate practices. Different process owners often make up their own rules as to how they select vendors and issue purchase orders. What ends up happening is that the purchasing people are unfamiliar with practices that have developed independently in various other departments. Conversely, the people in those departments are clueless regarding the rules and requirements that the organization has established for selecting vendors, placing orders, and monitoring supplier performance.

The substantial risk that accompanies some of these uncontrolled practices is that the organization will fail to monitor and gather pertinent information about critical suppliers for the simple reason that the suppliers are not recognized on the ubiquitous approved vendor list. This could result in finding out too late that a key supplier can't meet a delivery date or fulfill your requirements. Just because the supplier isn't furnishing components or raw materials doesn't mean it isn't important to your business.

As an auditor, I have on more than one occasion asked process owners if a particular supplier they use is on the company's approved vendor list, as described in their own procedure relating to supplier qualification. Invariably, I get a blank look and a shrug. Often, they aren't even aware that the company has a list of approved vendors. They are unaware of the company's purchasing procedure or if there is anything in it that pertains to their department's expenditures. The purchasing procedure is considered the property of the purchasing staff, even if they aren't the only ones doing the buying.

The purchasing personnel, for their part, have no idea who is authorized to buy materials and services that fall outside of their departmental boundaries. They may know that there's another form that is used, but they will often answer questions about supplier qualification with responses such as: "John in production handles that. It doesn't come through my office." Inconsistencies lead to practices that increase risk of miscommunication and organizational breakdowns that can cost the company time and money.

CONTROLLING THE PROCESS

ISO 9001 doesn't require you to have a purchasing procedure or an approved vendor list. It doesn't mandate that all buying goes through the purchasing function or that you limit your purchasing practices to one rigid method. What it does require is:

■ "Identify the processes needed for the quality management system and their application throughout the organization." (Ref: ISO 9001, 4.1 a)

■ "Documents needed by the organization to ensure the effective planning, operation and control of its processes . . . " (Ref: ISO 9001, 4.2.1 d)

■ "Evaluate and select suppliers based on their ability to supply product in accordance with the organization's requirements. Criteria for selection, evaluation and re-evaluation shall be established. Records of the results of evaluation and any necessary actions arising from the evaluation shall be maintained." (Ref: ISO 9001, 7.4.1)

■ "Determine, collect and analyze appropriate data to demonstrate the suitability and effectiveness of the quality management system.... The analysis of data shall provide information relating to . . . suppliers." (Ref: ISO 9001, 8.4)

Note that none of these requirements say: "The purchasing department shall..." The standard doesn't restrict the requirements to any particular entity within the organization. What it clearly intends is that the organization exercise appropriate control over any processes that affect organizational goals, regardless of where they may be situated within the mesh of interrelated processes that cumulatively define your QMS. Just because a department other than purchasing is buying something doesn't absolve the organization from the need to ensure that the suppliers are appropriately qualified and monitored.

It's important to look at what is being purchased. Are the suppliers furnishing product that is essential to the fulfillment of the organization's objectives? How critical are the materials or services that you are buying from them?

Listed below are some of the typical products and services that are either neglected or discounted when defining supplier qualification and purchasing practices:

- Contract/temporary labor
- Machine replacement parts
- Custom molds, fixtures, and stencils
- Independent test/validation
- Telecommunications equipment
- User manuals
- Vehicle leasing/fleet maintenance
- Off-site records storage

When writing your purchasing procedures or other documents you use to describe the procurement of goods and services, remember to include those processes that fall outside the direct purview of the purchasing department. Decide if your current practices are adequate and controlled. Is it more efficient for the organization to have only one process and require everyone to conform? Or is it OK to have three or four alternate methods, as long as they are defined, controlled, and effective? Is there a cost associated with having multiple methods? Is there a risk of breakdowns?

Sometimes, when departments are allowed to use their own processes for buying goods and services, they take shortcuts that can have consequences that they hadn't foreseen. It's also often the case that they are unfamiliar with some of the techniques that are used to ensure that suppliers have the capacity to fulfill requirements. If the company has auditors dedicated exclusively to assessing suppliers of raw materials and components, there might be value in having them mentor others in what to look for in a good supplier. Questions to ask (depending upon criticality to each unique organization) might include:

- Is the calibration house certified to ISO 17025?
- How does the temp agency qualify the people it sends?
- What records does the supplier keep?
- How does the customer survey specialist design the surveys he or she uses?
- How are customer surveys validated?
- Are the environmental monitoring gages at the remote storage site calibrated?
- How does the supplier monitor its critical suppliers—the ones whose performance could affect your delivery to your customer?
- What are the criteria for selecting an independent test lab?

The other consideration is that individual people often are responsible for only one part of the process. Their accountability may be limited to initiating a requisition or participating in an activity. For example:

■ Engineering may send out a prequalification questionnaire to potential suppliers whose products it is testing, initiating the ultimate selection process.

■ Shop personnel may fill out requisitions for tooling and get the appropriate signatures before forwarding them to purchasing.

■ A production manager might be the person most qualified to perform a site assessment of a new heat-treat or plating facility.

■ Accounting might have the most efficient access to the data needed to assess ongoing supplier delivery performance.

Regardless if you've decided to streamline everything into one procedure or to define and control as many processes as the organization deems appropriate, you must ask process owners what they do. People are often startled when they begin to list all the different things companies buy that are not funneled through the purchasing department.

To get a handle on how many people you may need to talk to, brainstorm your own list of possible purchases made outside the purchasing department. The list will include some of the items mentioned earlier in this chapter, but it may also include others unique to your industry. Once you have a comprehensive list, you can start finding the process owners. A good place to start is in the accounting department. If a product or service has been purchased, there's an invoice. If the purchase has been executed without a purchase order or comparable document, there probably will be a signature authorizing payment. Sometimes, it's the only control finance departments have over nontypical procurements.

Figure 2.1 includes a chart that will help you organize this assortment of suppliers and products that fall outside of the scope of the purchasing department. A blank form is included in appendix A.

The information that you gather will enable you to make informed decisions about whether suppliers need to be included in your process and what level of control might be appropriate. This worksheet helps you to accomplish several things.

Figure 2.1   Nonstandard Supplier and Product Worksheet

Supplier	Product/service	Department/ individual authorized to purchase	Criticality (5=most critical)	Customer required?	Comments
B-4 You Know It Delivery	Same-day delivery of packages	Customer service manager	3	N	Use for under 50-mile radius to deliver critical parts to customers
G&W Machine Parts	Standard off-the-shelf replacement parts for production equipment	Production manager, preventive maintenance supervisor	2	N	Multiple suppliers have same/similar parts
Buggy Pest Control	Pest control of warehouse and production area	Production manager	3	Y	Some customers are biomed companies; they require assurance that products will be free of insects, droppings, dander, and so forth
Livingston & Associates LLC	Developers of user manuals	Engineering manager, product manager	4	N	Write user manuals for new and revised designs
Customer-Comes- First Call Centers	Off-site call center to respond to customer complaints and inquiries	Vice president of sales	5	N	Represent company as point of contact with customer
Desk Set Office Emporium	General office supplies	Administrative staff	1	N	It's the only local supplier that stocks the cartridges for two of our older printers

This form allows you to list the process owners you've identified. Depending on how you ultimately decide to implement your process, you have a handy reference of all the players. This facilitates the defining of authorization and conformance with ISO 9001 requirement 5.5.1, which mandates that you define and communicate responsibility and authority. You may decide simply to insert the list of process owners into your purchasing procedure or solicit their help in developing a separate document that describes what they do. This same list may later be used to notify process owners of training on the organization's requirements relating to interactions with vendors. Even if they have a separate procedure, it's important for them to know things such as the established requirements for recording late deliveries, nonconformities, or other problems. They can be informed about internal mentors who can coach them on conducting on-site assessments or how and when to request a supplier corrective action.

The worksheet allows you to review criteria that will influence your decisions as to classification and category. You may even decide that a supplier's inclusion in the process isn't warranted. For example, the sample worksheet lists a pest control company. In some industries, the need to ensure that product is free of contaminants is a critical requirement. In those instances, having a reliable pest control service is important because customers have let you know that failure to provide evidence of an implemented process to ensure against animal droppings or dander anywhere on their product will result in your company's being disqualified as a supplier. On the other hand, the company that you buy your office supplies from probably doesn't need to be on the vendor list.

This example also includes a vendor that is specified by the customer. Just because a customer has told you that you must use a particular supplier doesn't absolve you of the requirement to qualify and monitor that supplier. At the very least, it will provide you with objective evidence in case the supplier's defects are the reason you miss your customer's delivery. Having information about the supplier that's independent of that which your customer has furnished also increases the likelihood that you'll be able to anticipate and better respond to any breakdowns that might occur. It may also present you the serendipitous opportunity to establish a relationship with a supplier you can use for other projects or clients.

Finally, having these suppliers on an accessible list ensures that if the regular process owner is away, the replacement or designee knows whom to call. For example, this chart lists a local courier for emergency deliveries. That information can be invaluable if a customer has a breakdown or a hospital needs a specimen tested.

At the end of this exercise you should have a list of the procurements made outside the purchasing department. You should be able to sort them into critical, important to monitor, good to be aware of, and irrelevant to the QMS. From there you can insert them into the matrixes that subsequent chapters will describe relative to categorizing, qualifying, and monitoring.

Chapter 3

Outsourced
Processes

C hapter 2 dealt with the purchasing process, giving special attention to those practices that occur outside the purchasing department. Many of those purchases are for outsourced processes. This chapter focuses on the relationship and controls of these outsourced processes, part or all of which are usually defined in a purchase order, contract, or similar procurement documentation.

WHAT IS AN OUTSOURCED PROCESS?

A great deal of confusion and a lot of discussion have surrounded the subject of outsourced processes. ("Outsourced processes" in this context does not necessarily refer to the practice of sending jobs offshore for cost savings. The definition is confined to that found in ISO 9001. However, in some instances, the result may be the same.) To allay some of the misconceptions, ISO/TC 176 published a guidance document to help organizations better understand the concept and the intent of the requirement found in subclause 4.1 of ISO 9001. It states: "Within the context of ISO 9001:2000 an 'outsourced process' is a process that the organization has identified as being needed for its quality management system, but one which it has chosen to be carried out by an external party." (ISO/TC 176/SC 2/N 630R2 ISO 9000 Introduction and Support Package: Guidance on "Outsourced Processes")

The outsourcing concept discussed in ISO 9001 relates to those activities essential to your quality management system (QMS) that are carried out by entities external to your organization. The standard requires the following: "Where an organization chooses to outsource any process that affects product conformity with requirements, the organization shall ensure control over such processes. Control of such outsourced processes shall be identified within the quality management system." (ISO 9001 subclause 4.1)

OUTSOURCED PROCESS REQUIREMENTS

Two distinct concepts are relevant to this ISO 9001 requirement. One relates to the notion that you can have a process that's essential to your organization but that's conducted, in whole or in part, outside of your facility. The other concept is somewhat implied. Because outsourced processes are generally paid for, it follows that those selling the service (i.e., outsourced process) should be qualified and monitored in a manner that is appropriate and comparable to that used for other suppliers. This is one of the methods—perhaps the most workable method—for fulfilling the requirements in 4.1 relative to ensuring control.

The outsourcing concept is included in subclause 4.1 of ISO 9001 to highlight the fact that special attention may be required when external organizations perform tasks that affect the quality of the products (and services) you provide to your customers. The requirement is situated in a part of the standard that doesn't allow exclusions; that's to underscore the importance of recognizing that an organization cannot absolve itself of accountability for how those processes are implemented and controlled.

Unfortunately, the misconception endures that it's permissible to abdicate responsibility for some of the processes that occur off-site. This fosters an underlying attitude in some organizations that the more remote the location of a process, the greater the justification for dissociating the process from the organization's QMS. All too often, auditors hear things such as: "We exclude 7.5.1 because we contract out the entire manufacturing process to another company." "We exclude purchasing, because that's done at corporate." "We don't do that here."

The question shouldn't be: Does it happen here or there? It must be: Is it a process that in any way has an impact on or " . . . affects product conformity with requirements"?

Geography is irrelevant. If, for example, the parts you design are fabricated in another country and then shipped back to you for distribution or sale, you have to define what control you have over the manufacturing process.

It doesn't matter if the process is conducted by another corporate office, a contracted service, or any other provider. The relationship between the organization and the supplier of the outsourced process is not an appropriate criterion for determining adequate control. For example, it's not uncommon for hiring and other human resource activities to be consolidated in one place for multiple divisions. The fact that qualification of candidates and maintenance of training records occurs at the sister division doesn't remove the requirement for the organization to define how those processes are controlled. Similarly, just because purchasing is done at another corporate location does not absolve the organization from the need to integrate control of this process into the QMS, most notably through the implementation of such clauses as 7.1 Planning of product realization: "The organization shall plan and develop the processes needed for product realization," and 4.1 "General requirements: The organization shall... identify the processes needed . . . and determine the sequence and interaction of these processes."

DESCRIBING THE SEQUENCE AND INTERACTION OF PROCESSES

This doesn't necessarily require the generation of a whole new set of documents. Some of the methods you can use to describe the sequence and interactions include the following:

■ Inclusion of the processes in the quality manual's section on interaction between processes
■ Reference in relevant procedures to internal or external documents that define the relationship and responsibilities
■ Description in process-related documents of the nature of the partnership, including how the outputs of these processes fit into the QMS.

Let's take a look at typical examples for each method.

■ *In the quality manual.* It's not uncommon for organizations to use a flowchart to fulfill the requirements of section 4.2.2 of ISO 9001 relating to the description of interaction of processes in the quality manual. Figure 3.1 illustrates an incomplete flowchart. The outsourced manufacturing process is excluded. Figure 3.2 demonstrates how the manufacturing process could be included to conform to the requirement of the standard. The outsourced process is included, and, for

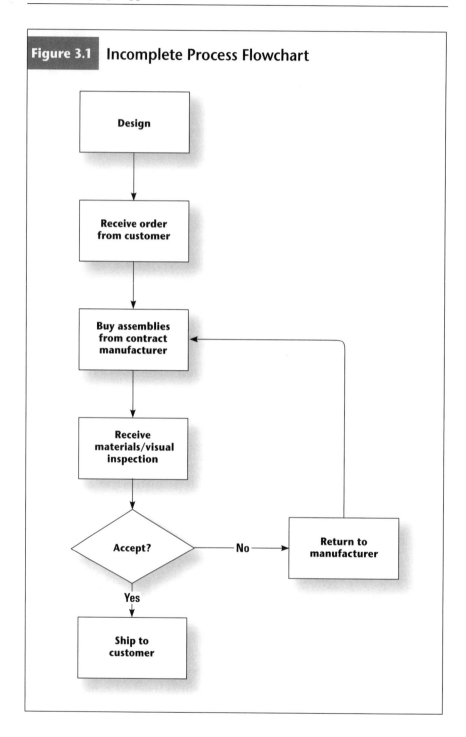

Figure 3.1   Incomplete Process Flowchart

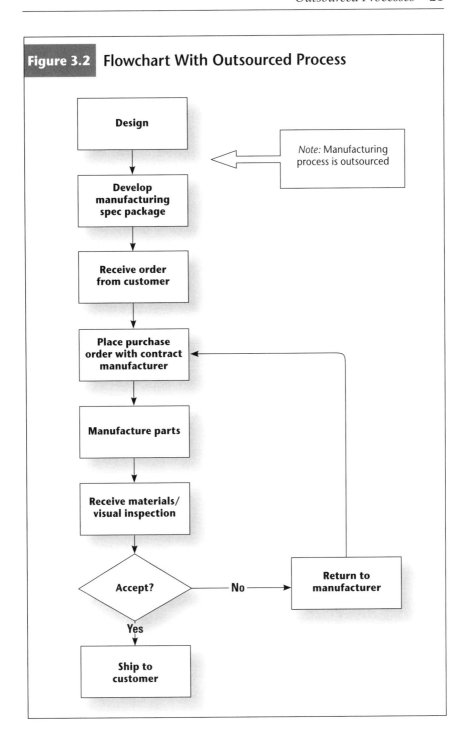

Figure 3.2   Flowchart With Outsourced Process

clarification, a brief note is inserted. The chart also defines part of the method of control in the box that addresses development of manufacturing documents. If the outsourced process is a major feature of the QMS, it should always be included in this flowchart, along with additional references in other documents.

■ *Reference in relevant procedures to internal or external documents that define the relationship and responsibilities.* In some instances, companies outsource only part of a process. They either don't have the equipment or have found it more cost-effective to have another company do it for them. Typical examples include special tests or processes such as heat-treat or plating. In these cases, it would be appropriate to refer to these activities within the text of the related production procedures or work instructions. The inclusion of the step in a production traveler (router) is often adequate. This has two added benefits: (1) It allows for the calculation of the off-site time of the material in the production schedule and (2) it prompts production and quality control personnel to verify that material is inspected or checked when it is received back from the vendor.

■ *In other process-related documents.* If a process is outsourced only some of the time, it might be more appropriate to identify the interface with other processes through a design process, a project management document, or a packet of customer specifications. In each instance, the document would identify where the activity fits into the sequence for the entire process.

These examples are intended solely to provide suggestions on how to describe the interaction and sequence of the processes within your QMS. They do not address the requirement in 4.1 of ISO 9001 relating to identifying the processes and describing the control.

DEFINING YOUR OUTSOURCED PROCESSES

What and how to control is dependent on the nature and complexity of the process. The controls must address such things as criticality of the process and the risks engendered. The criteria for all purchasing categories and the methods of qualifying the suppliers will be the subject of subsequent chapters. However, for now it's appropriate to remember that the outsourcing of a delicate machining process will probably require more vigilance than the purchasing of off-the-shelf components. This perspective will facilitate the decisions about when, where, and to what extent to define these processes within your QMS documentation.

What are your company's outsourced processes?

To be able to properly define outsourced processes, it's important to identify them and situate them within your QMS. A simple litmus test for any outsourced activity could be answering these two questions: Can you fulfill the customer's requirement without this process? And is your QMS complete without it? There are three ways of determining the answers to these questions:

■ Draw a flowchart illustrating the overview of the processes your organization conducts to bring product to market. (See figure 3.3.) These are your required processes. If any of them are done by a provider that is external to your organization, you have an outsourced process.

■ Consider if a particular activity is critical to your QMS. First example: Outsourcing the catering for the company's annual awards luncheon is probably not integral to fulfilling customer requirements. Therefore, it normally wouldn't be considered as a part of the QMS. (You could argue that it should be included if this is part of a recognition program relating to the organization's achievement of quality objectives. However, it's reasonable to exclude it). Second example: Outsourcing the development of the user manuals for your product is definitely integral to your customers' expectations and directly relevant to their ability to experience optimum value from the product. Also, it should be sequenced into the planning and design/development process, along with any related activities such as training service techs and field engineers, ensuring manuals are included in shipping documents, and incorporating provisions for review of any revision to the product.

■ Identify an activity and see if you can match it to any of the requirements in ISO 9001 (or any other QMS model that you use). From the examples given above we can easily identify the matches shown in figure 3.4.

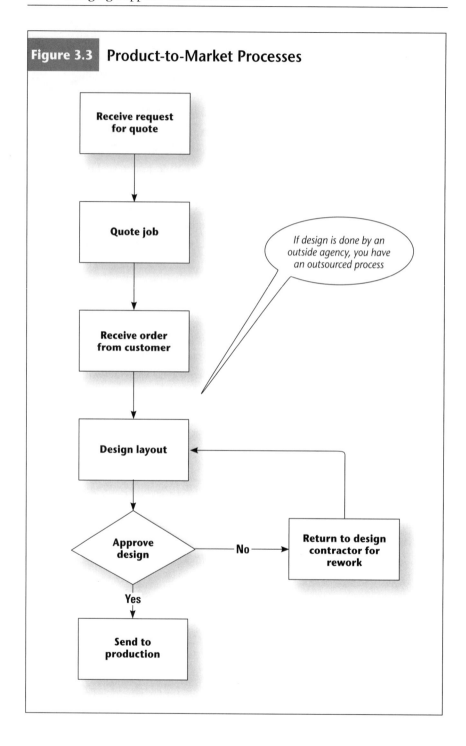

Figure 3.3   **Product-to-Market Processes**

Figure 3.4	ISO 9001 Activity Match		
Activity	**ISO 9001 reference**	**Requirement**	**Part of QMS?**
Design layout	7.3	Design and development	Y
Catering of awards luncheon	N/A	N/A	N
Development of user manuals	6.2.2, 7.1, 7.2, 7.3	Training, planning product development, additional requirements for product and design	Y

The reasons for outsourcing processes fall into two general categories: (1) The organization doesn't have the necessary expertise and resources; (2) the organization is able to perform the process but has chosen to outsource it for cost savings, increased efficiency, or some other business reason. Examples of typical outsourced processes include:

■ Design
■ Internal auditing
■ Calibration
■ Web hosting
■ Independent lab testing
■ Plating/painting/heat-treat/coating
■ Contract assembly (of components provided by the organization)
■ Entire manufacturing processes
■ Development of user manuals and maintenance instructions
■ Customer surveys (appraisals of customer perceptions)
■ Call centers
■ Design validation
■ Purchasing
■ Field service
■ Human resources
■ Preventive maintenance of equipment
■ Installation (where contractually required)
■ Records archiving

CONTROLLING YOUR OUTSOURCED PROCESSES

The diversity of processes that are outsourced illustrates why you must consider the manner in which each is controlled. It would be as inappropriate to use the one-size-fits-all approach for these processes as it would be for any other element of your QMS. The method used to plan how a part is manufactured is different from planning how an e-commerce Web site is set up. The tools and techniques employed to assess fulfillment and conformance of these two different requirements also would need to be quite different. In most cases, the control is achieved through a combination of several of the examples listed below.

Typical approaches for ensuring control over the outsourced processes include:

- *Supplier audit.* This is a very typical method for controlling outsourced processes. To ensure continued conformance to requirements, the audits are conducted at a frequency proportionate to the risk associated with the process. This is an example of a situation in which the qualifying and monitoring activities also serve as the method of achieving control.

- *Detailed process documentation, work instructions, build specs, guidelines, tooling, and so forth.* In some instances organizations provide specific documentation, not only on the product, but also on the manufacturing process. This would entail the development of all necessary work instructions and the provision of tools, jigs, and, at times, even the materials.

  The control need not apply only to complex processes. I've observed among several clients the outsourcing of simple, repetitive processes to organizations that provide training and work for people with mental and physical disabilities. These usually involve simple assembly, packaging, and sorting operations. The company ships these organizations all the required materials, sometimes including tools. They develop illustrations and easy-to-understand instructions. The trainers meet with the company to ensure they understand the process and then teach the members of their work force. Both organizations benefit from the arrangement, a manifestation of the eighth quality principle—mutually beneficial supplier relationships.

- *Third-party validation of product/process performance.* Into this category you can put products and processes that undergo scrutiny by a third party. This could be an independent lab, a company that contracts to do extensive testing, or a third-party expert (not unlike an auditor) who would do an assessment of either the product or the process capabilities.

- *Training.* The control of the outsourced process might be limited to providing the necessary training at the supplier's location. This might include allowing only those individuals qualified by your organization to work on your product. They would be required to demonstrate the necessary competence based upon your qualification criteria.

- *Joint planning sessions.* If the supplier is responsible for a large process (e.g., the manufacturing process for the module that constitutes half of your finished product), you will probably have ongoing meetings to coordinate all the activities and to ensure that all appropriate communications and interfaces are effectively carried out. This would include consideration of scheduling, inventory levels, engineering changes, document control, inspection/test criteria, addressing customer complaints, and so forth. You would have regularly scheduled meetings or conference calls, established protocols and contingencies, and extensive record keeping. The control of the process would be very "hands-on."

- *Representative on-site.* In this instance a representative of your organization works at the supplier's location, managing, overseeing, and sometimes even contributing to the work being done. This individual usually ensures that the process remains well controlled and that the outputs are acceptable.

- *In-process performance data.* At times, control can most easily and effectively be achieved by simply requesting regular data relating to process performance. This can include statistical process control (SPC) data, defect tracking, or a log of incidents that occurred during the manufacturing process. Coupled with this monitoring process would be a requirement for notification if there were a significant event or deterioration in the process capability.

- *Demonstrated conformance to ISO 9001 or comparable QMS model.* Sometimes registration to an ISO standard or comparable certification is adequate to ensure control. The best example of this would be a calibration house with an ISO 17025 certificate from an accredited body. Because the requirements for registration include the need for periodic surveillance, it's appropriate to assume that, as long as its certificate is current, it fulfills (and probably exceeds) your calibration needs. If you're going to rely on certification to an ISO standard to control any process, it's important to ensure that the certificate comes from an accredited source. (More on this subject in chapter 5.)

- *Preexisting criteria as defined in purchasing procedures.* In addition to all the methods described previously, companies may develop their own protocols for ensuring control of outsourced processes. Because of the enormous variety of organizations, there are probably dozens of other methods. Most of them will be directly relevant to the nature of the organization. Some may include consideration for regulatory requirements. The common denominator in all instances is the need to have defined, consistent, and effective methods for controlling the processes.

Some secondary activities also relate to the control of the output of the process. Generally, they don't suffice as "stand-alones" but are used in conjunction with the process controls listed previously. These might include:

■ Incoming inspection
■ Certificates of analysis
■ Final product conformance data

Finally, it's possible, and likely, that you'll use a combination of these methods to ensure adequate control.

These control mechanisms are generally defined and agreed to in a contract that's executed by the purchasing function or by individuals in the organization who are authorized to buy materials and services. Sometimes it's as simple as adding language to a standard purchase order. In other instances, it can involve extensive documentation. That's the link between the requirements relating to outsourcing and the ones relating to purchasing.

As with any requirement in a QMS, it's important that it make good business sense. What are the benefits that may be derived from outsourcing and from bringing definition, control, and consistency to these processes? The purpose of an activity is to fulfill the customer's requirement. If the outcome of such a process doesn't contribute to that purpose, it's a detriment. Having a supplier do something twice because it had poor control is no more efficient or less costly than if your organization repeats the processes. Both carry costs of scrapped material, lost time, wasted labor, missed deliveries, and customer dissatisfaction. Therefore, the benefits of definition, planning, control, and monitoring are the same . . . regardless of whether it happens here or there.

The criteria for selecting and monitoring vendors for outsourced processes will be discussed in later chapters, since this is often also the method used for controlling the processes.

Chapter 4

Classification
and Criteria

Before you can begin to qualify suppliers you have to know who they are and how important their contribution is to the fulfillment of your customers' requirements. Discussions in previous chapters have illustrated just how expansive and varied this group of stakeholders truly is. The risks that are engendered by each vendor, depending on the criticality of its product to organizational goals, are equally diverse.

Added to the considerations of product category are issues of criteria. These encompass concerns relating to cost vs. risk. Without criteria, qualification and monitoring activities become unwieldy and inefficient. This is inconsistent with the goal of responsible and cost-effective supplier management.

Very simply, not all rules will apply to all suppliers. The onus is on each organization to conduct appropriate deliberations upon the criteria and classification of its vendors. Without this sorting and filtering mechanism, organizations end up trying to apply one set of rules for all suppliers. This tactic varies from impractical to impossible, which leads to the kind of frustration that accompanies grudging adherence to a meaningless activity—and resentment for the "ISO thing."

Establishing classifications and defining criteria make it possible to realize optimum benefit from limited resources. Qualifying and monitoring a select group of suppliers, rather than having a generic scorecard for all, makes it possible to spend more time visiting, evaluating, sampling, and communicating with those companies whose products and services are most vital to your company. As with everything else, you get to decide which activities are appropriate to this process based upon the importance of each supplier to your organization.

What is critical to one company may be inconsequential to another. For example, purchasing soap for the company washroom shouldn't be a big deal (unless, of course, you run out). However, for a chain of upscale hotels or a fancy spa this is more than just a commodity. The quality of the soap can have a direct bearing on customer satisfaction. Just-in-time (JIT) is an example of a make-or-break requirement for many organizations. Delivery of specimens to a medical lab for presurgery screening relies on fast turnaround. It isn't just a matter of efficiency; it can make the difference as to whether the surgery can be performed.

For a company buying a part that's an off-the-shelf product, readily available from half a dozen local suppliers, the JIT requirement is probably a nonissue.

You need to know what these companies supply and how important the product is to your organization. Therefore, it's appropriate to expend the time needed to establish, develop, and implement your own supplier management process.

Classification and criteria allow you to group vendors and define sets of guidelines for each. Classification will relate to the types of products or services they provide. Criteria will relate to criticality of goods or services. In each instance, the classes and criteria will be dependent on your industry.

CLASSIFICATION

Categories can generally be divided into the following:
- Raw materials
- Components
- Tooling
- Services (calibration, equipment maintenance, field installation)
- Outsourced process (e.g., manufacturing, test, design, packaging)
- Infrastructure
- Miscellaneous/supplies

You may choose to identify subdivisions such as:
- Components:
  - ☐ Production stock
  - ☐ Made-to-order parts
  - ☐ Repair department inventory

- Infrastructure:
  - ☐ Production machinery
  - ☐ Telecommunications equipment

The categories may have some overlap. Field installation may be a purchased service that is, coincidentally, also an outsourced process. In another instance, the organization may contract with the supplier of a piece of capital equipment to also do the annual maintenance on the machine or provide refresher training for operators. When you're classifying these suppliers, put them into the category that makes the most sense for your organization.

The last category looks as if it might be filled with the least critical suppliers—the ones you don't have to worry about. That's not an invalid assumption. However, some things might be put into this category simply because they don't fit in any of the others, but they're still important. Examples might include epoxies with finite shelf life, replacement electro-static discharge (ESD) wrist straps, specially treated paper for clean-room environments, mobile document shredders, and so forth.

Categories help identify the stakeholders and process owners in your organization who have decision-making authority. They'll also identify the individuals who will be affected by the output of the purchasing process—in other words, the users of the product or service. They in turn can provide further information about the criticality of the product. Or they may be able to furnish pointers on what to look for when selecting and qualifying a supplier. For example, the inspection department supervisor will know, based upon such things as usage, types of instrumentation, and customer requirements, what kind of calibration services are warranted. This can include consideration for frequency, certificate requirements, and whether to use serial numbers or other company-assigned identification codes, and so forth. The purchasing manager then has the *specification* for the product (in this case the product is a service) that is being purchased. Therefore, it's useful to know who the user of the product is.

Classification into categories gives you a clearer perspective on your particular assortment of suppliers. (See figure 4.1.) It lets you cull the vital few from the insignificant many so that you can use your limited resources where they're most needed. It lays the foundation for planning your supplier qualification and monitoring activities. As in any other process, good preparation and planning ease implementation. Bear in mind that although many of the categories are typically associated with manufacturing, every company has suppliers.

Figure 4.1   Classifying Suppliers in Categories

Supplier	Category	Criticality (5=most critical)	Qualify/ monitoring code — Initial	Qualify/ monitoring code — Ongoing	Customer requirement?	Comments
B-4 You Know It Delivery	Service				N	Local delivery of critical parts to customers
Buggy Pest Control	Service				Y	Required by biomed clients
Chemicals-R-Us	Raw materials				N	Resins and dyes
Customer-Comes-First Call Centers	Outsourced process				N	Outsourced customer-call center
Desk Set Office Emporium	Miscellaneous				N	Local supplier, stocks cartridges for older printers
G&W Machine Parts	Tooling				N	Replacement parts for production equipment
Golly-Gee Gizmos	Components				N	Machine and build subassemblies
Livingston & Associates LLC	Outsourced process				N	Write user manuals
The Archive Depot	Outsourced process				Y	Record storage—customer-mandated and specified
Zip-Zap Inc.	Components				N	Distributor, generic parts

Supplier Qualification and Monitoring Matrix

Distributors, Manufacturers' Representatives, Brokers, Wholesalers

Before we continue to criteria, one group of companies deserves additional mention. These companies actually can fit into more than one category, depending on the products they sell. They are the enterprises that occupy the place in the supply chain between manufacturers and end users. The descriptions below aren't absolute but more general in nature. It's possible that manufacturers may have different arrangements with their distributors and wholesalers. The purpose of discussing them is to provide guidance in assigning criteria and to ensure their appropriate inclusion in your supplier management process.

When considering criteria and classification, distributors and similar businesses seem to somehow get exempted from the supplier qualification and monitoring process. It's common practice for purchasing personnel to excuse distributors from the vendor assessment requirements they apply to most of the other companies they do business with.

The defeatist notion that prevails is that distributors are impotent go-betweens with no appreciable influence on the product. Many distributors perpetuate this view by implying, either deliberately or inadvertently, that if the manufacturers they represent are ISO 9001-certified, then the blessing somehow rubs off on them, too. And conversely, if there's a problem with a product or the manner in which it's delivered, the fault lies not with the distributor but with the manufacturer. What ends up happening is a shell game in which no one is accountable.

The actual consequences of this mind-set are troubling. Distributors are routinely added to the ubiquitous approved vendor list (AVL) without any assessment or qualification. Rarely is there a set of criteria for qualifying distributors. When there's a problem with defective product or late deliveries, requests for corrective action aren't sent out. It's automatically assumed that since the distributor didn't manufacture the product it either won't respond or won't be able to take any meaningful action to address the matter. The smaller distributors beg off, insisting that they have little or no clout. They abdicate responsibility and their customers absolve them.

Distributors play a vital role in industry. They serve the market by providing local access to varied products. Good distributors provide product support and facilitate inventory management. Many of them have achieved ISO 9001 registration.

However, the customers they supply still look to the manufacturing source for answers to problems that arise. The function of the distributor is either discounted or viewed as an obstacle. That's unfortunate.

When an organization buys a product from a distributor, the activities that are involved in fulfilling specified requirements originate with the distributor. The factors that distinguish one distributor from another really aren't the product lines they carry. The distinctions relate to the manner and level to which they serve their customer base—in other words, how they control their processes and implement their quality management system (QMS).

Activities and factors that relate directly to a distributor's influence on your ability to fulfill your customer's requirements may include:

- Customer service and order-taking processes
- Warehouse personnel's ability to recognize product when pulling orders
- Packing and shipping practices
- Minimum/maximum levels, purchasing practices
- Shelf life of certain commodities
- ESD protocols for electronic components
- Availability of current literature
- Relabeling, packaging, or other value-added processes
- Ongoing training for new products
- Traceability and lot control
- Control of nonconforming material
- Document control (contracts, material safety data sheets, certificates of analysis, electronic infrastructure)
- Corrective action program.

It's even appropriate to conduct on-site audits if the product the distributor is furnishing is critical to your product. Questions that you may want to ask to qualify a distributor might include some of the following:

- How does it double-check orders to verify that the shipping documents match the customer's order?
- How are special instructions communicated?
- Does it participate in the periodic training that some manufacturers offer?
- How does it control materials that are environmentally sensitive?
- What are the monitoring procedures for products with limited shelf life?
- Does it substitute different manufacturers' products without notifying you?

(This is not an uncommon practice; substitutes are routinely furnished unless a customer stipulates otherwise).

■ How does the organization ensure it can meet customer delivery requirements?

■ What process does it have in place to handle nonconforming product?

■ What is the procedure for inspecting material that has been returned before it's put back in stock?

■ Who is responsible for corrective action?

These questions can be asked informally or in conjunction with the audit checklist found in chapter 5. Answers to these questions will provide insight into the overall control the company has over its critical procedures. It will also reflect the extent to which it recognizes its own accountability in the supplier chain.

Other factors that affect your distributor include mergers with other companies, relocation, acquisition (or loss) of product lines, and turnover in personnel, to name just a few. When a merger occurs, manufacturers have to assess if they will allow the distributor to continue to carry their product line if the newly formed company now also represents their competitors' products. Or, if a large distributor spins off a small division, the manufacturer may determine that the newly spun-off company doesn't have the resources to represent it effectively in the marketplace. The opposite scenario might increase a distributor's product offerings and present you an opportunity to consolidate purchases. But without periodic monitoring, most of these changes won't come to light—until there's a problem. If the products you're buying from distributors are critical to your ability to serve your customers, it's appropriate to ask them to furnish evidence of their license/permission to sell a manufacturer's product line.

Manufacturers' representatives serve a similar function. The chief manner in which they differ from distributors is that they usually don't inventory product. They sell goods, offer technical assistance, and communicate with the manufacturers on your behalf. They have less overhead than distributors do but may also have less clout than distributors because they don't invest in inventory.

Brokers do carry inventory but rarely have contractual agreements to represent a manufacturer's product line. They typically buy excess inventory, overstock, obsolete components, or parts that may still be good but have expired warranties. They may buy product that is perfect except for packaging, or they may acquire inventory from a bankruptcy or foreclosure. In most cases there is absolutely nothing wrong with the goods they are selling. They fulfill the customers' requirements for fit, form, and function. In some instances brokers might do all the research you don't have the time to do and find the distributor that has the components you desperately need.

Good brokers will be up-front with you about the as-is condition of product and its limited or expired warranty status. They provide a great service. Sometimes manufacturers make parts obsolete with little or no notice, leaving you with a giant hole in your production schedule because your design won't work with the recommended replacement. In that case, brokers may be the only ones who know where to get the parts you need.

Wholesalers are the middlemen in the chain between manufacturers and retailers. They function much in the same way as distributors do, except they do so in the consumer marketplace rather than in the industrial arena.

The bottom line is: Organizations must establish criteria for distributors, manufacturers' representatives, brokers, and wholesalers just as they do other categories of suppliers.

CRITERIA

Setting criteria for classification boils down to risk. How vulnerable is your organization if something goes wrong with this supplier? How much of the total material that goes into your finished product is purchased from any particular vendor? What kinds of things could go wrong and what impact will that have on your organization—on your ability to serve your customers?

Criteria, like classification, must also be tailored to your organization. This brings control to the process of defining risk and criticality. Whereas classification addressed various sort of suppliers by product, such as components and services, criteria evaluate them based upon importance. Consider the following three vendors. They all provide a transportation-related service. In all instances we are dealing with vehicles. Depending on the nature of your business, the processes related to the use of the vehicles, and contractual agreements with customers, the ratings will be significantly different.

■ Leasing company that provides you a fleet of delivery trucks
■ Service company that provisions and maintains bloodmobiles
■ Local garage that services the company vehicle used for errands

If a company delivers almost all its orders to its customers, maintaining its fleet of trucks is a big deal. If its product is perishable, it's an even bigger deal. On the other hand, if the trucks are small, generic, and easily replaced when there's a problem, the risk associated with this service is important but not critical.

The second example involves very specialized vehicles equipped with delicate instrumentation and refrigeration units. The consequences of losing all the blood collected during a blood drive is gigantic. The vehicle also probably needs to comply with statutory/regulatory rules. Finally, these vehicles aren't easily replaced and if one broke down, it's possible that a planned blood drive would have to be cancelled.

The third example illustrates the folly of having no criteria for qualifying and monitoring suppliers. It's always a good idea to have any vehicle running efficiently and to maintain the value implicit in this asset. But this one isn't critical to fulfillment of customer requirements or organizational goals. If you need to run an errand and the company car is in the shop, you can borrow someone else's or use your own. Having the garage mechanic on the approved vendor list just clutters the process.

Although the preceding examples present extreme applications, they do illustrate the need to consider the criticality for suppliers in all categories. Otherwise, there's a risk of discounting a candidate whose failure could seriously hamper your company.

What follows is a discussion of various criteria that organizations may wish to consider. The answers that result from the exercise will give you guidance for the next chapter, which deals with methods of qualifying and monitoring suppliers.

Examples of Criteria

■ *Dollar volume.* How much money do you spend with any particular supplier? The answer to this question leads to other concerns and additional questions. It allows you to reflect on more than just your vulnerability in case something goes wrong. It also indicates to you which companies you may wish to forge stronger alliances with. If the dollar volume of purchase orders is high, it's fair to assume that you are a significant customer to the supplier and that it will be more attentive to your requirements. Of course, the assumption doesn't necessarily work if you're a small player in a very large industry.

The fact that you're buying a lot of material from the supplier might also suggest that it traditionally has reliable products and good delivery performance. Therefore, you're able to rely on the supplier and perhaps are even willing to make concessions to enjoy favored customer status.

What risk does this relationship hold? Because of volume, do you have a special payment agreement? If the supplier merged with another company, and that agreement were nullified, how serious an impact would it have on your cash flow? If it went out of business, could you find alternate suppliers for its product?

The other interesting outcome from looking at vendors based on dollar volume is the decision to exclude some of these vendors from contention as high-priority risks. Organizations discover that the list of high-dollar payments is often headed by utility companies and financial institutions. Although they definitely have a role to play in the fulfillment of organizational goals, they probably aren't contenders for semiannual surveillance audits. Nor will they be included in the list of suppliers selected for analysis of on-time delivery. This again illustrates the drawback of having one single, unqualified list for all vendors.

- *Percentage of the finished product.* This criterion is similar to the one relating to dollar volume. It's not unlikely that they will be one and the same. However, it's possible to have one supplier provide most of the components or raw materials, but not necessarily the most expensive ones, that go into your product. Will you be able to find alternate sources easily if anything should happen to this supplier or to your relationship with it? The risk in this case is comparable. But the answers may be very different. The parts may represent a large percentage of the overall complete product, but if they are mostly generic commodities available from several reliable distributors, this would lower their criticality rating.

- *Cost of component.* Expensive components are often also those that have longer lead times, are less likely to be stocked because of their value, and less easily substituted if something goes wrong. How reliant is your product on this one high-priced component? If the answer is that it won't function without it, then the criticality rating for this supplier should be high.

- *To-specification versus off-the-shelf.* It stands to reason that you want to exercise more care in selecting suppliers that will make product to your specifications. You need to be assured of their ability to manage your documentation (including care for proprietary information) and of their ability to understand your requirements and acceptance criteria. They must be able to respond quickly to engineering changes. Good and consistent communication practices are requisite. Depending on the quantity of parts being fabricated, this criterion should usually rate high and warrant at least an initial qualifying audit.

■ *Lead time.* If the product you're buying has a long lead time, you must be assured that you aren't going to wait six months to receive something that doesn't match your requirement. Depending on risk, this criterion should usually get a rating similar to the to-specification criterion.

■ *Handling of processed or customer-owned material.* The criticality of this feature is proportional to the value of the parts being furnished. It's also dependent on the risk that the outsourced process carries. If parts are being packaged, then the risk of damage is low. If, however, they are being plated, welded, etched, and so forth, then the risk of ruining the product is significantly higher. The other consideration is that you're entrusting the supplier with the care of a product that's owned by your customer. The supplier must demonstrate its ability to control the process and also conform to your requirements relative to the handling of customer-owned materials.

■ *Sole source.* Just because a supplier is considered a sole source for a product or service doesn't mean you don't have choices. Organizations often feel at a bargaining disadvantage when dealing with suppliers of exclusive products. You may have to buy from them (for now) but you can do several things to ensure that they fulfill your requirements. You can learn as much as you can about them through audits and research. You can attempt to forge a stronger relationship or establish processes that are mutually beneficial. You should monitor their performance. If the analysis of data reveals that they are contributing to problems, you have the objective evidence to get management to allocate more resources to find an alternative or to get engineering to redesign the product. If you're thrilled with the performance of sole-source suppliers, that's great. If they're a headache, remember: Nothing lasts forever. But you can't be a catalyst for change unless you have objective data. Don't use the excuse that they are a sole source to omit them from qualification and monitoring activities.

■ *Customer-specified.* Everything that applies to sole source applies to this category. Just because customers specify certain vendors doesn't mean you shouldn't monitor them. If they're the reason you keep having defects or missing deliveries, the objective evidence from analysis of performance data is your strongest ally when dealing with your customer.

■ *Criticality of service.* Most of the categories so far have dealt with components and materials. It's also important to consider the criticality of services. Remember, some of the suppliers that harbor the greatest risk aren't the ones that provide materials. Don't forget the company that hosts your Web site, the independent test lab that validates your product, the temp agency that furnishes you with contract workers during your rush season, the telecommunications giant you depend on to communicate with customers around the world, and the printer who produces your owners' manuals—to name just a few. If the integrity of a test lab's results is questioned, what will it mean for the product that you've sent out to several thousand customers? How much of your business comes from e-commerce and how vulnerable are you to problems with the outfit that maintains your Web site?

■ *Responsiveness.* How quickly does the supplier respond when you call? Does it sell a product that requires contingencies for emergency containment, recall, or notification? How fast does it turn around a request for a quote? How many people staff its technical support lines? How important is it that you can work with the supplier easily?

Implicit in all the listed criteria is the fact that the levels and kinds of risk will vary greatly. How big is big? How bad is bad? You get to decide.

Some suppliers may represent more than one risk, amplifying your organization's vulnerability. To sum up, when rating criticality, you must assess the criteria for magnitude. Additional appropriate considerations will be:

■ Are you really at risk if you have a lot of money tied up with one supplier?
■ Are there any alternate sources?
■ What will it cost to replace or repair damaged parts?
■ How much time is lost if parts are defective?
■ What's your vulnerability if the supplier goes out of business?
■ How bad will it be if the supplier is late delivering?
■ Will you really antagonize the customer if you use another source?
■ How great is your exposure?
■ How large is the risk?
■ How many different risks does one supplier pose?

The ratings in the following matrix run from one to five. (See figure 4.2.) Nothing is magical about the numbers. Try to achieve consensus when assigning a number to a supplier. General rules for using the matrix are:

■ If you can't decide between two numbers, go for the higher one. You can always back off later.

■ Customer-mandated suppliers should never go below a three. This is an implicit feature of the ultimate product you deliver.

■ Instead of totally excluding a company, consider putting it on the list and giving it a rating of one. In the example in figure 4.2, the office-supply company is included just so that there can be a note about where to find the old-style cartridges.

■ Suppliers in the same category may get different ratings. In the example, although two companies both technically furnish components, one is a distributor while the other does fabrication and assembly.

Once you've assigned your suppliers a criticality rating, you can decide what methods you will use to evaluate them and how you will monitor them.

Figure 4.2   Rating Criticality

Supplier Qualification and Monitoring Matrix

Assign a rating based on magnitude of risk →

Supplier	Category	Criticality (5=most critical)	Quality/ monitoring code		Customer requirement?	Comments
			Initial	Ongoing		
B-4 You Know It Delivery	Service	3			N	Local delivery of critical parts to customers
Buggy Pest Control	Service	3			Y	Required by biomed clients
Chemicals-R-Us	Raw materials	5			N	Resins and dyes
Customer-Comes-First Call Centers	Outsourced process	5			N	Outsourced customer-call center
Desk Set Office Emporium	Miscellaneous	1			N	Local supplier, stocks cartridges for older printers
G&W Machine Parts	Tooling	2			N	Replacement parts for production equipment
Golly-Gee Gizmos	Components	5			N	Machine and build subassemblies
Livingston & Associates LLC	Outsourced process	4			N	Write user manuals
The Archive Depot	Outsourced process	3			Y	Record storage—customer-mandated and specified
Zip-Zap Inc.	Components	3			N	Distributor, generic parts

Chapter 5

Supplier Qualification

The manner of evaluating and qualifying a supplier depends on multiple factors, including the nature of the product it furnishes, the criticality of the product, and the interaction between your two organizations. A distributor of generic commodities may sell its products through a Web site, receiving thousands of orders daily from you and your competitors. Another company may execute an ongoing contract to service a fleet of delivery trucks. Companies that have only one customer will have predictably greater involvement and more frequent interaction with their sole client. You might contract with machine shops that fabricate parts to your specifications and software companies that design programs to your defined requirements. Some operate within your facility; others are halfway around the world. All these factors play a role in deciding the methods that you will use for qualifying and monitoring your suppliers.

The qualification process also allows you to identify opportunities. Once a supplier is identified and has been evaluated, it's possible to explore other services that might be contracted or additional products that you might want to buy from it. It's not uncommon during a supplier audit to discover that the supplier's product offerings and capabilities exceed what you originally assumed.

The same tools you use for initial qualification may also be used for monitoring, reevaluation, and requalification. You may decide that a supplier is so critical that you will conduct an initial qualification audit and then periodic audits every six months. Or you may choose to do only one audit to establish the vendor's capabilities and then use analysis of performance indicators for ongoing monitoring.

The method you choose depends on such factors as the industry, type of product, and the nature of the relationship. For example, raw materials are more essential to a chemicals plant; components, to an assembly house.

The classification and rating of criticality you've already done will be helpful. The other consideration is constraints. For example, it would be wonderful to have a team of supplier auditors visiting every single supplier that you think is important. However, time, money, and staffing rarely accommodate that kind of commitment.

It isn't practical to visit all suppliers. In our global economy, it's becoming increasingly challenging to find local vendors. A company may have rated a five on your criticality chart, but it's on the other side of the world. As a matter of fact, you may have suppliers on several different continents. Which ones will you visit? Have you allocated money in the budget for travel expenses? Do you have auditors who can make long trips several times a year? Conversely, if you decide that you won't be conducting audits of offshore suppliers, what alternate method will you use to qualify them—to ensure that they can consistently meet your needs?

The same constraints exist even if your suppliers are domestic. Do you have enough trained auditors? Will they have time to conduct the audits? How will you qualify the suppliers if you won't be conducting audits?

What follows is a brief discussion of the more popular methods for qualifying suppliers. The list doesn't reflect any particular ranking or consideration of criticality.

Methods of qualification:
- Vendor self-assessment
- On-site audit
- On-site visit
- Historical/anecdotal evidence
- Past performance (grandfathering)
- Receipt of samples
- ISO 9001 (or comparable) registration
- On-site inspection/product release

VENDOR SELF-ASSESSMENT

Vendor self-assessments are an efficient method of gathering information about company capabilities, product offerings, services, size, special technologies, and commitment to quality. If you have a large number of vendors, this method is most useful, especially if you have limited resources. It also can serve to identify and prequalify suppliers that will later require an on-site audit. The information on the self-assessment form will also help you to prepare for the audit.

For this method to work, you must give appropriate consideration to the following factors.

Vendor Self-Assessment Survey

Develop a form that includes the information that's important to your organization. Generic forms are readily available, but they sometimes omit significant questions. A sample form appears in this chapter. (See figure 5.1.)

Define frequency

How often will you send the forms out? Will you use them only for initial qualification or will you send them out periodically (e.g., every two years) to ensure that information remains current?

Action if supplier doesn't mail it back

What action will you take if a supplier fails to return a vendor self-assessment? We've already discussed the fact that purchasing is often done by many functions. What happens if engineering has selected a new vendor for a critical component in a new design and you are having trouble getting the vendor to respond? If suppliers have the latitude to ignore requests without consequence, you may have to reconsider the effectiveness of this method for qualification.

Ensure communication to relevant personnel

Ensure that the request is routed to the correct person at the supplier's facility. Sometimes the failure to respond is a simple matter of miscommunication—in other words, the contact person never received the request.

Record retention

Where will the returned vendor self-assessment forms be kept? The two typical functions that share responsibility for these records are purchasing and quality assurance. It's appropriate to consider which choice is best for your organization. Purchasing maintains direct interface with the supplier and is the function that needs to know vendor status. However, quality assurance personnel often have more experience in assessing the information to determine how well it reflects process capability.

Figure 5.1   **Vendor Self-Assessment Survey**

Company		Date_____ / _____ / _____
Address		
Phone		**E-mail**
Fax		**Web site**
President		
Quality manager		
Production manager		

Please furnish the following information:

1. ISO 9001-certified? (Please furnish copy of certificate.)

2. If not ISO 9001-certified, do you comply with ISO 9001 or any other recognized quality standard? (Specify.)

3. Summary of facilities and capacity. Include information relative to size of manufacturing area, number of employees, equipment technology.

4. Product(s) or service(s) supplied. Include brochure, catalog, or promotional literature.

5. Ability to furnish certifications or traceability of products or services supplied?

6. Average lead time for standard products

(continues)

Figure 5.1	**Vendor Self-Assessment Survey** (cont.)
Do you:	**Comments:**
☐ Have a quality manual? (Specify last revision date.)	
☐ Maintain a document control system?	
☐ Have controlled procedures for relevant functions? (List major functions defined in procedures.)	
☐ Have a process for maintaining customer documents and specifications?	
☐ Perform incoming inspection?	
☐ Perform final inspections?	
☐ Segregate and identify nonconforming material?	

Do you:	Comments:
☐ Have a calibration system?	
☐ Have an approved vendor list?	
☐ Have a preventive maintenance program for production equipment?	
☐ Conduct internal audits?	
☐ Have a process for addressing corrective action requests?	

(continues)

| Figure 5.1 | **Vendor Self-Assessment Survey** (cont.) |

Additional comments or information

Authorized signature: _____ Date:_____/_____/_____

To be filled out by purchasing supervisor or quality assurance manager.

☐ Approved   ☐ Conditionally approved   ☐ Not approved

Comments:

Signature: _____ Date:_____/_____/_____

ON-SITE AUDIT

The supplier audit is one of the most proactive and thorough means of assessing an organization's ability to fulfill your requirements reliably and consistently. It gives you the chance to look at not only the supplier's product but also its processes. You have the opportunity to observe how it conducts its business and to determine what good practices it has in place to ensure its consistent ability to fulfill your requirements.

Chapter 6 provides more in-depth information about supplier audits.

ON-SITE VISIT

A site visit isn't the same thing as an audit. It can be used as a preassessment or simply to acquaint yourself with the managers and key personnel of the business. It often includes a tour of the facility, demonstration of special capabilities, and a presentation by the sales staff. It may even be appropriate to request evidence of financial stability. Again, it's not a formal audit.

If a vendor doesn't have the criticality to warrant an audit, it might be appropriate to ask some of the same kind of questions found in the audit checklist to gain enough knowledge to qualify it. The report that comes out of the visit should provide a summary of what was learned and if any tentative agreements were made.

HISTORICAL AND ANECDOTAL EVIDENCE

If an organization has a sterling reputation in the marketplace, you may decide that this provides adequate criteria for qualification. If you belong to an association that shares information of this nature or have respected colleagues who attest to the reliability of suppliers, you may choose to qualify them based on your associates' recommendations. Testimonials, trade journals, and published surveys can also be used as reliable indicators of supplier capability.

PAST PERFORMANCE (INCLUDING GRANDFATHERING)

"Grandfathering" means the practice of qualification, inclusion, or exception from rules based on past performance. The practice was widespread in many organizations certifying to ISO 9001:1994. It was an end-run that they believed allowed them to absolve themselves of the need to do any qualification or monitoring.

ISO 9001:2000 did a better job of expressing requirements for qualifying and monitoring suppliers, including the addition of language referring specifically to analyzing data relating to suppliers. You may have originally placed multiple suppliers on the approved vendor list based on the grandfathering rule, but now they get to stay on only if they meet established criteria.

Past performance (or simply performance) then becomes the criterion for maintaining qualification. The indicators of performance will be discussed in chapter 7.

RECEIPT OF SAMPLES

Sometimes the only way to really tell if a company can meet your requirements is by looking at actual examples of its work. This could be either because of the complexity of the product or because of the peculiarity of your own requirements. Either way, you must decide what your acceptance criteria will be. The shortcoming of this method of qualifying is that you have limited knowledge of the supplier's processes and, therefore, limited ability to gauge reliability and repeatability.

ISO 9001 (OR COMPARABLE) CERTIFICATION

Certification to ISO 9001 or one of the comparable quality management system (QMS) models is an excellent method of qualifying suppliers. It's at the heart of the certification industry. The fundamental principle is that these standards define a minimum set of near-equivalent and interchangeable criteria to which all organizations must subscribe to demonstrate their ability to meet customer requirements. They create parity in the marketplace and give everyone the same set of basic playing rules. So you should be able to rely on that certification to qualify your suppliers.

You must bear in mind a few provisos and eventualities.

ISO 9001 certification doesn't guarantee that an organization meets *your* organization's quality requirements.

You may have additional requirements that exceed those found in the standard. These may relate specifically to your product or involve regulatory mandates with which you're required to comply. If that's the case, using just the ISO 9001 certificate won't ensure that the supplier can get the job done for you.

Certificates Expire

If ISO 9001 is the only criterion you have for qualifying your suppliers, you must be vigilant about expiration dates. If a company has lost its certification, it's doubtful it will send you a memo to alert you to that fact. Ask for renewal certificates.

Certificates Cover a Specific Scope

Make sure that the certificate the company gives you includes the product you want to buy. Whether innocently or deliberately, it's possible for a potential vendor to send you a certificate that represents only one segment or division of its business. Review the scope of the certificate.

Certificates Don't Necessarily Transfer in Mergers

If a company is sold off to another enterprise or becomes an independent entity, the original certificate does not transfer. Similarly, if a business is acquired and becomes wholly owned by another company, the acquiring party may not then claim ISO 9001 certification for its entire organization.

ON-SITE INSPECTION AND PRODUCT RELEASE

Sometimes the best way to determine if a company can meet your needs is to be physically on-site when the prototype run comes off the production line. To do this, the acceptance criteria must be specified in a contract or purchase order. You would probably use this method in those instances in which a product was being manufactured wholly to your company's specifications. It might be done as a follow-up to an on-site audit and in anticipation of awarding a large contract. It will probably also include validation of the manufacturing process.

OTHER CONSIDERATIONS

Based upon the criticality and nature of the suppliers, your requirements, and your available resources, you can now decide what methods of qualification you will apply to your suppliers. Some additional factors and constraints that will come into play include:

Geographic Location

Sometimes it simply isn't possible to conduct an on-site audit. In our global economy, it's not unlikely that some of your key suppliers will be on another continent. You must weigh the cost of travel against the risk of dealing with potentially incomplete or skewed information. You can sometimes solve this by contracting with an independent agency in the other country to conduct the audits and submit reports.

Corporate Division/Subsidiary

If the supplier is another division of your organization, you may decide to forgo an audit. However, if the components or service are critical to your product, you might try to negotiate an even swap of internal auditing so that both facilities reap the benefits of an objective assessment.

Availability of Auditing Staff

You may have 40 suppliers that you'd like to qualify using a supplier audit. However, you have only three auditors and they spend most of their time doing internal audits or working on improvement initiatives. This means you need to set priorities and decide which companies you will audit.

Provisional Qualification

To make more efficient use of your resources and to address scheduling concerns, you may choose to prequalify suppliers or give them provisional status based upon your initial assessment.

CHOOSING A METHOD

Finally, for each method you must define and control what forms you will use, if applicable, to whom the information will be reported, the type and location of records, and appropriate follow-up actions.

Based on category and criticality, you can assign a qualification code. This will indicate the method you will use. What follows is an example of possible codes. (See figures 5.2 and 5.3.) In each case you have the option of two methods for each code. This helps to resolve issues relating to limited resources. It also addresses the fact that some methods are more appropriate because of the nature of the product or service being provided. (See figure 5.4.)

You may choose to use only one method or to combine two or more. For example, you could start with the self-assessment as a precursor to the on-site audit or use the ISO 9001 certificate for provisional qualification and then wait for a sample order to be fulfilled.

Figure 5.2 **Qualification Codes**

Code	Methods	
A	On-site audit	On-site inspection/product release/process validation
B	ISO 9001 (or comparable) certification	Site visit
C	Vendor self-assessment	Receipt of samples/incoming inspection
D	Past performance	Historical/anecdotal evidence

Figure 5.3   Supplier Qualification and Monitoring Matrix

Supplier	Category	Criticality (5=most critical)	Quality/monitoring code		Customer requirement?	Comments
			Initial	Ongoing		
B-4 You Know It Delivery	Service	3	C		N	Local delivery of critical parts to customers
Buggy Pest Control	Service	3	C		Y	Required by biomed clients
Chemicals-R-Us	Raw materials	5	A		N	Resins and dyes
Customer-Comes-First Call Centers	Outsourced process	5	A		N	Outsourced customer-call center
Desk Set Office Emporium	Miscellaneous	1	D		N	Local supplier, stocks cartridges for older printers
G&W Machine Parts	Tooling	2	D		N	Replacement parts for production equipment
Golly-Gee Gizmos	Components	5	A		N	Machine and build subassemblies
Livingston & Associates LLC	Outsourced process	4	B		N	Write user manuals
The Archive Depot	Outsourced process	3	B		Y	Record storage—customer-mandated and specified
Zip-Zap Inc.	Components	3	D		N	Distributor, generic parts

Figure 5.4   Comparison Chart of Qualification Methods

Method	Benefits	Drawbacks
Vendor self-assessment	■ Easy ■ Provides good basic and easily verifiable information ■ Practical, convenient form	■ Dependent on veracity of supplier ■ Subject to differing interpretations ■ Not appropriate for high-risk requirements
On-site audit	■ Comprehensive assessment of supplier capabilities	■ Time-consuming ■ Dependent on availability of auditors ■ Travel expenses
On-site visit	■ Assess general condition of company	■ Informal and subjective ■ Impractical for remote suppliers ■ Not necessarily indicative of capacity or capability ■ Not appropriate for high-risk requirements
Historical and/or anecdotal evidence	■ Easy ■ Reliable	■ Subjective ■ Not appropriate for high-risk requirements
Past performance	■ Easy ■ Often substantiated by some form of records	■ May not reflect current capabilities ■ Limited in information provided ■ Not appropriate for high-risk requirements
Receipt of samples/ incoming inspection	■ Demonstrates quality of product	■ Provides no information about quality of process ■ Not appropriate for high-risk requirements
ISO 9001 (or comparable) certification	■ Reliable benchmark of quality ■ Easy to request from supplier	■ May not be indicative of your requirements
On-site inspection/ product release/ process validation	■ Real-time evidence of product acceptability ■ Reassurance of process capability	■ Time-consuming ■ Not always an option ■ Not appropriate for some products/services

The Supplier Audit

Supplier audits provide an opportunity to acquire valuable in-depth knowledge about organizations that substantially influence your ability to serve your customers. You get the chance to thoroughly and objectively assess how they conduct their business and determine if the quality management system (QMS) they have in place is adequate to ensure their ability to meet your needs.

SUPPLIER AUDIT CRITERIA

Organizations must establish criteria for deciding which suppliers (and potential suppliers) will be selected for on-site assessments. It's neither warranted nor appropriate to conduct audits for all of your suppliers. The time and resources expended should depend on the criticality of the product or service each supplier provides. Otherwise, resource constraints will inevitably cause the supplier audit program to degrade into an uncontrolled haphazard activity typified by rushed audits, rescheduling, and ineffective visits conducted by unqualified staff. Eventually the process is simply abandoned.

It's better to do fewer audits, targeting the suppliers most important to your organization. In this way you can use the good auditing practices that will ensure that you get the most benefit from the visit. This can't happen if the process is unplanned, overburdened, or poorly implemented.

Supplier audits should be conducted by trained, qualified auditors using industry-recognized auditing practices, established guidelines, and in accordance with the auditor code of ethics. This isn't a casual visit. It's an audit. It has structure, rules, and protocol. An audit is a controlled process. As with any other process, it should be characterized by the same features: definition, planning, inputs and outputs, resources, qualified personnel, records, and measurement. Audits rely on objectivity, documented criteria, and verifiable evidence. The output of this process is the audit report, accompanied by requests for corrective action when appropriate.

SCHEDULING

Audits aren't surprise events. They should be properly scheduled at a time that's convenient to both parties. You want the auditee's attention during the audit and the opportunity to speak with key personnel. That's difficult to accomplish if you're vying for time and access with visiting customers, end-of-month production push, vacation schedules, or the annual picnic. Your organization's time is too precious to be squandered on an unproductive audit that won't provide the requisite information. To minimize the risk of an ineffective audit, schedule the audit and confirm the date several days before your visit.

Supplier audits should be conducted in the spirit of the ISO 9001 quality management principle of "mutually beneficial supplier relations." You need the product the supplier sells; it (like you) needs customers. One of the results of the audit will be either a decision to approve a supplier or to maintain its qualification on the approved vendor list. The audit should, therefore, provide objective evidence to support the decision. It also provides the opportunity to communicate to an organization what it must do to become a qualified supplier. For periodic reassessments, information that may be collected will relate to such things as increased capacity, change in product offerings, decrease in staffing, mergers, increased outsourcing, acquisitions, or new technology.

Suppliers should know ahead of time what the scope of the audit will be. If they have multiple product lines and facilities, you may limit the scope to the area that's most relevant to your organization. You may also decide to do a process audit and focus on only one process or on a clustered group. For example, if you're outsourcing your heat-treat to a company that also does plating and machining, you may choose to look only at the heat-treat and the ancillary processes.

ESTABLISHING REQUIREMENTS

It's also important to tell the supplier which standard or requirements you will use for the assessment. Audits must be conducted against a documented set of requirements. These can be:

■ Its own internal procedures, a copy of which you must receive ahead of time

■ The international standard it is certified to—in other words, ISO/TS 16949, AS 9100, and so forth

■ Any applicable regulatory requirements

■ Your procedures

If you're going to be using either your own procedures or an industry standard, you must ensure that the supplier has the relevant information. Otherwise, you must furnish it in advance so the supplier can determine if it's able to meet your requirements. This could save you a trip if it reviews the requirements and has to concede that it would probably fail your audit.

AUDIT CHECKLIST

To make the most of your limited time, it's essential to have prepared a checklist. You don't need to show it to the supplier in advance. These are your guidelines. In addition to providing a framework for questions, checklists furnish an organized format for taking notes that will make report writing more productive. (See figure 6.1 at the end of this chapter.)

Checklists are also useful if you have an auditor-in-training or if you've included a technical specialist on your audit team. Use of technical experts who aren't trained auditors is warranted if the auditee has complex or specialized processes that require assessment by a person with comparable expertise.

For the sake of efficiency, some organizations use one generic checklist from which they add and subtract items as appropriate. This isn't a bad idea, provided that you review the checklist before arriving at the supplier's location.

If you are using a scoring checklist, it's a courtesy to share it ahead of time. This kind of checklist assigns numerical values to the auditee's level of conformance to requirements and is intended to remove bias. Because it's primarily used for awarding major contracts, sharing the checklist with the potential supplier before the audit lets it know what the rules are for winning the bid. Some regulatory bodies also use scoring checklists.

Scoring checklists may bring more objectivity to decision making, but I find them daunting for the auditee and constraining for the auditor. I'm not a proponent of their use.

Your audit checklist should be planned to elicit the information that you need. Not all categories are relevant to all suppliers. A visit to the organization that is bidding for the contract to do aftermarket field service will differ from the visit to the company that's furnishing resin for your molding process. In each instance there are processes that are of greater importance to your organization. In the first case, communication with customers and technicians' qualifications may be critical, whereas in the latter, information about raw-material traceability, equipment preventive maintenance, and statistical process control may be of greater concern. Always make sure to include questions about document-control and record-retention practices. These are the two common denominators in all organizations.

PLANNING THE AUDIT

Plan your supplier audits with thoughtful deliberation so that the results benefit your supply chain management processes. Don't forget supporting activities that may be directly relevant to the organization's ability to meet your requirements. As appropriate, include questions relating to such things as identification, labeling, packaging, inspection, calibration, aftermarket support, response time, and inventory levels.

The questions you ask have the added benefit of communicating to the supplier the features of its QMS that are most critical to your organization. If you're not asking questions about how the supplier handles these features, the tacit message you're sending is that these are things you don't particularly care about.

Ensure that there's enough flexibility built into your audit plan so that you may skip some processes if you have time constraints or so you can add things if you become aware of additional activities or areas of concern.

AUDIT REPORTS

After the audit, write a report. It should state what your assessment of the organization is based upon the standard you used. It should mention strengths, examples of good practices, descriptions of features or special processes that are of particular importance to your organization, areas of concern, and actual nonconformities. You may specifically state what improvements you must see to award a contract or to continue doing business with the supplier. You must provide a conclusion as to your assessment of the vendor's ability to meet your organization's requirements.

Make sure that you provide the supplier a copy of your audit report. All audits, regardless of their purpose, scope, or source, should provide you with information that leads to greater knowledge about your organization and opportunities to improve. Your suppliers should reap the same benefit from your audit. You may send them either the audit report that you retain for your own records or a separate report edited for their use.

Supplier audits are one of the best tools an organization has to establish a foundation for mutually beneficial supplier relations. Definition, planning, and control ensure that the process has value. Consistent implementation relates directly to the integrity of your supply chain—and your sustainability.

Figure 6.1   **Supplier Audit Checklist**

Company		Auditor(s)		Date of audit
Address		ISO Certificate?		If yes, scope?
Phone	E-mail	Products		
Fax	Web site			
President		Purpose of audit		
Quality manager		☐ Prequalification		
		☐ Qualification		
Production manager		☐ Periodic visit		
		☐ Requalification		

Description	Documentation used Procedure, work instructions, other documents	What are you trying to verify? What kind of evidence will you look for?	Comments and evidence Evidence or other objective means to determine level of compliance to requirements (When an item of activity is not applicable to the organization being audited, please make note in this area or mark "N/A."
Management responsibility			
Quality policy? Mission statement? Objectives?		Does it have a mission statement or quality policy, indicating the company's commitment? Does it have published goals, objectives, targets, projections that are communicated to everyone in the company?	
Organizational chart?		Does it have an organizational chart or other document that defines responsibility, chain of command, direct reports, who does what?	
Review of quality system Quality system Quality manual		In the absence of an ISO 9001-based system, is there evidence of strategic planning, risk management, analysis of resources, problem solving, and so forth? What is management's level of awareness of the status of various processes?	

(continues)

Description	Documentation used	What are you verifying?	Comments and evidence
Quality system			
Quality manual		Does it have a quality manual, and what does it include?	
Control of data and documentation			
Documented procedures and processes		What kind of documents, work instructions, SOPs, manuals, and guidance documents has the supplier developed for its processes? (Assess their adequacy.)	
Approval, access, legibility		Are the procedures and so forth that it is using approved? Do they appear to be current? Any obsolete documents? More than one revision being used? Accessible? Legible?	

Description	Documentation used	What are you verifying?	Comments and evidence
Control of revisions and customer specifications		How does it control customer drawings and specifications (including packaging, delivery, and any other specs)? How does it handle design and engineering changes, revisions, and deviations?	
Electronic documentation		How much data are held electronically? How are the data protected? Password access? Is the system backed up? Is all information that must be protected included in the backup process?	
Records		As you go through each area or process, assess the adequacy, accessibility, and general condition of quality records. Consider: ■ Receiving ■ Inspection and test ■ Certificates of analysis ■ Certificates of calibration ■ Completed routers ■ Training ■ Corrective actions ■ Status of nonconforming material ■ Contracts/purchase orders	

(continues)

Description	Documentation used	What are you verifying?	Comments and evidence
Resource requirements			
Equipment		Can the supplier tell you its production capacity? Does it have adequate machinery? Does it have redundancy (i.e., more than one machine that does the same thing)?	
Preventive maintenance		Does it have a maintenance program? What kind of records does it keep of equipment performance?	
Personnel		Adequate number of individuals qualified on each machine, function, or task (including customer service)? Method of qualification?	
Training		What kind of training? Cross training? Any industry or regulatory-mandated training? Certificates of off-site training?	

Description	Documentation used	What are you verifying?	Comments and evidence
Purchasing			
Suppliers evaluation documents and records		How does it evaluate suppliers? Does it conduct audits? Does it subcontract any processes? Does it track performance?	
Approved vendor list		Does it have a list? Are service providers, such as calibration houses, test labs, and so forth, on the list? When was the list last updated?	
Purchase order information		What kind of information does it require on purchase orders? How are POs generated?	

(continues)

Description	Documentation used	What are you verifying?	Comments and evidence
Customer orders			
Quoting process		Verbal quotes? Records of quotes? Authority to sign quotes? Policy in case of revisions or changes (requote)?	
Verification of requirements		How does it check to make sure that it has all the information it needs to process an order and that it matches what was quoted?	
Processing of orders Adding to production		Electronically? Given to one person who enters them? Authority and responsibility? How are orders handed off to production—or shipping?	

Description	Documentation used	What are you verifying?	Comments and evidence
Handling and communication of special requirements		Consider packaging, labeling, serializing, handling, shipping, and so forth.	
Customer approval First-piece acceptance		Does it have a mechanism for conducting first-piece inspections and getting customer approval?	
Handling or changes to orders		Quantity, delivery, cancellations, and so forth?	

(continues)

Description	Documentation used	What are you verifying?	Comments and evidence
Inventory and storage			
		How are inventory data kept? How is raw material identified? Lot traceability? How are finished goods identified? General condition of warehouse?	
Inspection			
Incoming		What are the criteria for acceptance of raw materials, components, materials? How is verification recorded? Sampling plans used?	
Process control			
Define production sequence		Does it use routers? Travelers? What defines the sequence of operations?	
Production schedule		What drives the production schedule? Who controls the schedule? How well can it respond to an emergency or rush order?	

Description	Documentation used	What are you verifying?	Comments and evidence
Verification of individual processes (identify each, including test, inspection, acceptance methods)		In this section, select manufacturing (i.e., product realization) processes and assess their adequacy and how they're controlled. Include verification/product-acceptance processes for each, as applicable.	
(1)			
(2)			
(3)			
(4)			

(continues)

Description	Documentation used	What are you verifying?	Comments and evidence
Final inspection			
		What are the criteria for final product acceptance? What is the mechanism for releasing the product for shipment?	
Shipping			
		How well controlled is the shipping process? Packaging, protection of product? Company fleet of trucks or common carriers? Certificates that accompany shipments?	
Control of nonconforming product			
Segregation		Does it segregate nonconforming product?	

Description	Documentation used	What are you verifying?	Comments and evidence
Identification		Is it properly labeled or marked to ensure against unintended use? How?	
Disposition		Does the supplier record what it does with the material?	
Measuring and test equipment			
Calibration schedule		Does it have a schedule for calibration? Are process equipment gages (such as pressure gages) on the schedule? Is there any test software? Are there test jigs that need to be periodically assessed for wear?	

(continues)

Description	Documentation used	What are you verifying?	Comments and evidence
Calibration stickers (or alternative method)		How are calibrated instruments identified? Can production people distinguish between reference tools and calibrated ones?	
Records and certificates		Are certificates of calibration available? Do they identify the standard used for the verification? Do they have traceability?	
Procedure for calibration		If the supplier does in-house calibrations, does it have documented instructions?	

Description	Documentation used	What are you verifying?	Comments and evidence
Preventive action			
FMEAs		Does it conduct FMEAs (failure modes and effects analysis)?	
Risk management		How does it assess risk and the potential for problems? What contingency plans does it have?	
Corrective action			
Customer complaints		Are formal corrective actions used to address customer complaints?	

(continues)

Description	Documentation used	What are you verifying?	Comments and evidence
Root cause analysis		Is it investigating the root cause of problems?	
Corrective action plans		Is it defining and carrying out an action plan for corrective action?	
Follow-up		Is it verifying results of CARs?	

Description	Documentation used	What are you verifying?	Comments and evidence
Internal auditing			
Audit program		Does it have an internal auditing program?	
Schedule		Is it conducting internal audits at defined frequencies?	
Trained auditors		Are the auditors trained?	

(continues)

Description	Documentation used	What are you verifying?	Comments and evidence
Audit records		What kind of records does it have of audits? How are the records used? (Trace back to management. . . .)	
Analysis of data and statistical techniques			
What data analyzed		Is it analyzing/measuring any processes or features?	
Data collection		Does it use SPC? What other methods does it use to track data?	

Chapter 7

Purchasing Tips

The information contained in the previous chapters is of limited value if it doesn't support your purchasing activities. It's great to be able to identify, sort, classify, and qualify your suppliers. But when all is said and done, you need to get down to the business of actually buying stuff.

The qualification that you have undertaken, coupled with the monitoring that will be the subject of the next chapter, are dynamic, ongoing processes that should continually provide you with current information about the status and capability of your suppliers. Additionally, if you conduct on-site audits, you should also garner information that will actually make some of the decision-making process easier. You may have learned about a company with priority services or a supplier that has just acquired a new test facility. On the other hand, you may have become aware of a reliable vendor that, because of downsizing, won't be able to handle the large-volume purchases you are anticipating in the coming year but that will continue to be a good source for short runs.

Obviously, you've been purchasing for years. The categorized list of suppliers isn't new. Many of the vendors have already been qualified. You aren't establishing a brand-new department from scratch. What you're doing is bringing consistency and definition to your purchasing process to improve your customers' satisfaction and your company's bottom line.

Your goal is to continually work at optimizing your supplier base using various criteria that may change through time for each product or service. Once you have selected the organization you'll be ordering from, the next thing to consider is the manner in which you communicate your requirements. Every order placed is a contract between you and your supplier. It's a documented statement of requirements. The better job you do of communicating what you need to your suppliers, the better they can serve you.

This is the flip side of the customer-supplier relationship. Consider how frustrating it is for you when a customer complains that you haven't delivered the product the customer anticipated and you realize it's because there were several expectations that hadn't been adequately defined. The situation is awkward because you both know that:

■ The customer didn't clearly state the requirement.

■ You made some inappropriate assumption because of the lack of clarity—in short, you guessed.

Rather than getting into a pointless blame game about accountability, it's best to resolve to address the root cause of this problem and develop purchasing processes that will ensure that you, as the customer, don't impede your supplier's ability to serve you.

PURCHASING DOCUMENTATION

What follows are tips on what to include in your purchasing documentation to ensure that those requirements are adequately understood.

Product Requirements (Including Service Contracts)

Ensure that the specifications are clear and complete. Include part numbers, revision numbers, exceptions, and any additional information required. If the contract is for a service, make sure that the requirements and deliverables reflect what was discussed and include any applicable contingencies.

More is better when it comes to product information. Don't assume that the vendor will know what you want. What happens if your regular contact person is on jury duty and you have to speak with a temporary replacement who is unfamiliar with your account?

Resist the temptation to take shortcuts, especially with critical information. Stating "Same as previously furnished" can get you in trouble if you've ordered multiple times and have also revised the specifications sometime during the life cycle of the product. Although suppliers should review specifications, being unclear about requirements or revision levels hampers their ability to determine what you really want.

If you're ordering from a catalog, double-check the part number. If the catalog is more than a year old, verify that the part number and specification haven't changed.

Secondary Processes

When sending parts out for plating, cutting, heat-treat, and so forth, make sure that paperwork accompanies the material. This shipment generally has a lot of value added into it already because of multiple machining operations. If the supplier makes a mistake because your information was incomplete, the loss is not only the raw material but the cost of all the time and labor that has also gone into the material.

If the supplier will need to use a print, send one along; don't assume that it has the one you sent with the original request for quote (RFQ). This is especially true if you tend to make a lot of revisions to parts.

Industry Standards

It's not uncommon in some industries for there to be acceptance criteria that are either commonly recognized or described in an industry-specific publication. The IPC standard relating to electronics includes, for example, illustrations on acceptable solder connections. For other industries there are a plethora of criteria for things such as pixels, flash, perpendicularity, opacity, trace elements, pizza delivery time, standard tolerances, cleanliness, and so forth. It's important that you determine two things:

■ Does your supplier conform to the accepted industry practices?
■ Do your requirements exceed or in any way differ from the conventional industry norms?

This is another example of something you might determine through an audit or a vendor self-assessment.

If the attribute is critical to your application, ensure that you have the industry specifications that describe acceptance criteria.

Delivery

Make sure the delivery requirement makes sense. Don't plug in the date you enter the order for as the due date to send a subliminal message that you want the parts "now."

Insert a delivery date that is reflective of your actual requirement and/or the best date you've been able to negotiate with the supplier.

Having accurate delivery requirements brings more reliability to the data relating to supplier performance. If you have no idea when you really need stuff, how can you possibly assess if your suppliers have been effective in meeting your requirements?

Ensure that there is consistency within your organization as to what the "due date" really means. Is it:

- A default date that signifies nothing?
- The date you wanted the material?
- The negotiated date your supplier said it could fill your order?
- The date when the last item on your purchase order will be received?
- The date the material leaves the supplier's facility?
- The date the product arrives on your shipping dock?
- The new promise date someone entered and updated when the supplier let you know it couldn't make the original date?

Sometimes, purchasing software limits the choices as to what date you can input. This is especially true if you have multiple line items with several release dates. In this case, if you have limited control over the data, ensure that you have consistency of interpretation about what the data mean. If individuals don't agree on what the due date actually reflects, the resulting analysis of supplier performance will be unreliable—and may even prove to be seriously flawed data. And if you're relying on that data to make decisions about which suppliers to keep on your approved vendor list, you could easily jeopardize a good partnership.

Additional Requirements

Labeling, packaging, certificates of analysis, beta testing, on-site inspections, and aftermarket tech support are all examples of requirements that must be clearly specified in the purchase order or contract.

The criticality of the requirement should influence your decision as to its placement on the purchase order. If something is important, it shouldn't be buried in boilerplate language or fine print on the back of the order form. Highlight it; put it in bold print; insert the text within a distinctly noticeable border. It's unfair to expect your suppliers to scrutinize orders looking for any special requirements. After all, they may receive hundreds of orders daily from companies that all have their own ordering formats.

Ensure there is consensus in your organization as to where and how special requirements are indicated on purchase orders.

It may also be important to specify the format for accompanying documents and records. Do you have your own verification checklist that you would like the supplier to fill out before shipment? Do you require evidence of final review before the completion of a design project? Would you prefer that certificates of analysis be mailed to you or do you want them enclosed with the shipment of raw materials?

Some organizations have a separate document that specifically addresses packaging and shipping requirements. These are generally furnished once to the supplier and then referenced on its purchase orders (for example, "Ref. XYZ Company Document 17-111 for Shipping and Packaging. Use Code 311 for labeling and Code 432 for packaging.") If you use this kind of document, take the time to do a periodic audit to ensure the information remains current. If it changes, make sure to let your suppliers know. They can't do the right thing if you don't tell them your rules have changed.

Electronic Media

Ensure that you understand how your vendor's Web site works. The increase in efficiency that both parties enjoy through the advent of e-commerce is sometimes balanced by the loss of that "personal touch." You can't easily override things such as minimum order value or standard-sized packaging. If the vendor's Web site states that orders processed after 2:00 p.m. will go out the following day, then you can't expect overnight delivery if you order something at 2:15 p.m. Being aware of the constraints ahead of time diminishes the risk of disappointment caused by unanticipated contingencies.

If you're having trouble navigating a Web site or placing an order, notify the supplier. It needs to know about these glitches that are affecting your ability to do business with it.

When using EDI (electronic document interchange) and other electronically controlled programs for minimum/maximum inventory levels, bear in mind that the data are only as reliable as the human beings who enter them. Things change; make sure the data keep up.

Amendments

Ensure there is consensus in your own organization about how changes to purchase orders and contracts are documented. Do you generate a change order, simply amend the original order in the system, or make notes on a hard copy?

If you accept changes that suppliers (and customers) authorize through e-mails, make sure that those e-mails don't remain locked in one person's password-protected in-box. Establish protocols for where the e-mails go so that they are accessible to authorized personnel, remain secure, and can be easily retrieved when needed.

Identify who is authorized to change contracts and purchase orders. Sometimes it's even important to ensure that your supplier knows who in your organization has the authority to amend a contract.

Remember that any changes to specifications include the aforementioned tips on communicating requirements.

Don't forget to complete the loop by revising any related documents and by communicating changes that can affect your delivery to your customer.

If you know ahead of time what your suppliers' capabilities are, you can better match them to your requirements. And, if you communicate those requirements clearly and adequately you help to ensure that they will be able to fulfill them.

Chapter 8

Supplier Monitoring

Once you've set up companies in your supplier database or added them to your approved vendor list, you need to decide what you will do to ensure that they continue to be able to fulfill your requirements. The methods you use for periodic monitoring will resemble those used for initial qualification. However, you may decide, for example, that after having done an initial audit, you will maintain their qualification status based solely on their performance. Or, you may have other suppliers that are so critical that you will continue to audit them every six months.

QUALIFICATION METHODS

What follows is a discussion of the qualification methods as applied to the monitoring process.

Vendor Self-Assessment

You may require companies to resubmit self-assessment forms periodically, for example every three years, so that you can determine if there have been any significant changes in their organizations.

On-Site Audit

Certain critical vendors will warrant periodic audits. In some industries, such as medical device and aerospace, this is a very common practice. It's good to remember that during a follow-up or periodic audit, you may discover that their capabilities have changed. They may have acquired new technology or lost the use of a critical piece of production equipment. They may have had to restructure their business and now have a smaller technical support staff or have decided to outsource a process that you consider critical to your product. Supplier auditing isn't about looking for problems and defects. It's about assessing an organization's ongoing ability to fulfill your requirements. It should also make it possible for you to recognize additional opportunities.

On-Site Visit

Once you've established a supplier, it's unusual to go back for another visit. In a few instances this method could serve as part of the ongoing monitoring process. If you're involved in a joint project or some other partnership, a debriefing (sometimes called a postmortem) is appropriate. A meeting is held in which each party's performance is discussed in a forum that allows for the generation of meaningful data. This is an appropriate tool for deciding whether to continue the relationship with the supplier and partner with it on future projects.

The only other viable reason for a second informal visit to a supplier might be if it acquires new technology and invites you to come see its increased product offerings or process capabilities.

Historical and Anecdotal Evidence

Like the on-site visit, the informality of this method limits its value for continued monitoring. Once you've established a vendor, you'll want more objective evidence to verify its continued capability. Besides, you will have developed a history with the supplier and so your reliance on the recommendations of others fades away.

Past Performance (Grandfathering)

Grandfathering also fades into memory, but it's replaced by various performance indicators. The majority of your ongoing monitoring will be in the performance indicators category.

Receipt of Samples

This category also will fade away, replaced by more measurable performance indicators.

ISO 9001 (or Comparable) Certification

This method has limited value for continued monitoring since renewals are generally on three-year cycles. However, it's important to be vigilant about requesting copies of new certificates when they are issued, since you are, in essence, relying on the registrar (or other certifying authority) to periodically assess the supplier's conformance to a recognized standard. Finally, for some suppliers continued certification may be absolutely essential to your organization. For example, you may have a customer that requires you to use an independent test lab with an ISO 17025 certification. If the lab loses its certificate, you could fail to meet one of your client's contractual requirements.

On-Site Inspection and Product Release

Because this method is very product-specific, it may be used every time a new product comes off the line. It may be the case that for one or two suppliers—and only in certain industries—this would be the most appropriate tool for assessing continued qualification.

PERFORMANCE INDICATORS

The kind of data you gather about suppliers depends on the nature of the product and its criticality to your ability to serve your customers. For example, you may choose not to monitor on-time deliveries for all your suppliers. Delivery information on the organization that comes in twice a year to calibrate your instruments would usually be meaningless. You call; it comes. It calibrates stuff, sends you certificates and an invoice, and then leaves you alone until you call again.

As with so many other things, there's usually a caveat. If you're a large manufacturing facility with hundreds of devices and you subcontract the entire calibration process to an outside provider, your risk level goes up. If you rely on the provider to keep track of when things are due and it misses a three-month cycle, then you

Figure 8.1	Monitoring Codes	
Code	**Methods**	
A	On-site audit	On-site inspection/product release/process validation
B	ISO 9001 (or comparable) certification	Site visit
C	Vendor self-assessment	Receipt of samples/incoming inspection
D	Past performance	Historical/anecdotal evidence

could find yourself in serious trouble during an audit. However, unless you have this kind of arrangement, it's fair to assume that keeping delivery information on the calibration house is a waste of time.

For your more critical suppliers you may decide to use more than one method. You could require evidence of continued certification to ISO 9001 plus various data on key performance indicators.

The supplier qualification and monitoring matrix you've developed to categorize and classify your vendors will be useful to you. (See figure 8.2.) You'll also want to reference the chart you created for qualification codes. (See figure 8.1.) As with the initial qualifying process, you have a choice of at least two methods for each level, with the flexibility of moving up or down depending on criticality and constraints.

You can't perform the same level of monitoring for all your suppliers. It's wasteful and pointless. Bringing some sanity to this process ensures that you expend your limited resources on monitoring the suppliers that engender the greatest risk for your organization. To bring uniformity to the process of selecting methods for monitoring, it's appropriate to create a coded grid to provide guidance. The "D" indicates performance monitoring; the numbers coincide with the criticality column from the supplier qualification and monitoring matrix.

The chart in figure 8.3 illustrates the kind of coding you may choose to establish. It uses information that you assembled as you were developing this process.

You'll notice that you don't bother to do any monitoring of some suppliers. As the criticality of the suppliers' products and services increases, the level and complexity of the monitoring increases. There's usually an inverse ratio between criticality and the amount of monitoring. The companies requiring the most monitoring will represent the smallest percentage of your total supplier base. If you look

Figure 8.2 Supplier Qaulification and Monitoring Matrix

Insert monitoring

Supplier	Category	Criticality (5=most critical)	Qualify/monitoring code		Customer requirement?	Comments
			Initial	Ongoing		
B-4 You Know It Delivery	Service	3	C	D	N	Local delivery of critical parts to customers
Buggy Pest Control	Service	3	C	D	Y	Required by biomed clients
Chemicals-R-Us	Raw materials	5	A	A–D	N	Resins and dyes
Customer-Comes-First Call Centers	Outsourced process	5	A	B–D	N	Outsourced customer-call center
Desk Set Office Emporium	Miscellaneous	1	D	D	N	Local supplier, stocks cartridges for older printers
G&W Machine Parts	Tooling	2	D	D	N	Replacement parts for production equipment
Golly-Gee Gizmos	Components	5	A	A–D	N	Machine and build subassemblies
Livingston & Associates LLC	Outsourced process	4	B	B–D	N	Write user manuals
The Archive Depot	Outsourced process	3	B	B–D	Y	Record storage—customer-mandated and specified
Zip-Zap Inc.	Components	3	D	D	N	Distributor, generic parts

Figure 8.3	Examples of Performance Indicators to Monitor

Code	Performance indicators to monitor

D–5	■ Results of periodic supplier audits
	■ Formal tracking of product nonconformities
	■ Formal tracking of delivery
	■ Formal tracking of complaints and problems relating to:
	  ☐ Failure to respond to requests for corrective action
	  ☐ Nonresponse to queries and requests for technical support
	  ☐ Nonfulfillment of additional quality requirements relating to certificates,
	    reports, labeling, traceability, packaging, and so forth

D–4	■ Formal tracking of product nonconformities ■ Formal tracking of delivery ■ Recorded problems relating to delivery, tech support, miscommunications, and so forth, as noted in comment field on approved vendor list
D–3	■ Formal tracking of product nonconformities ■ Recorded problems relating to delivery, tech support, miscommunications, and so forth, as noted in comment field on approved vendor list
D–2	■ Only recorded problems as noted in comment field on approved vendor list
D–1	■ None

at the supplier qualification and monitoring matrix, it's apparent that only part of the list falls under the D-4 or D-5 codes, and only two of those have been identified as candidates for periodic surveillance audits.

The sample chart was designed to reflect many different kinds of suppliers. In actuality, probably a much larger percentage will fall into the D-3 through D-1 codes. In the typical organization with 200 or so suppliers, the number of suppliers requiring high levels of monitoring is probably between 15 percent and 20 percent of the total. Of that number, perhaps less than half will warrant audits. As with all things, these estimates completely depend on the nature of your individual business.

Product Quality

This is probably the most important indicator of your suppliers' ability to serve you. Defective, nonconforming, or not-as-expected product causes you to miss deliveries to your customers, waste time either reworking material or sending it back, and disrupts your organization. It's also inherently the performance indicator that reflects how often your customers got bad parts because of a supplier error, or how many times nonconforming material almost made it out the door. This indicator also evokes the most visceral response from managers. No one likes to deal with the cost, risk, and disruption caused by bad product.

Bear in mind that if you are buying a service, then the nonconformity will relate to the terms of the service agreement. If you needed reports sent in a particular electronic format and they get mailed to you in hard copy, you have received nonconforming product from that vendor.

Delivery

Getting perfect product three days late is another source of costly disruptions. It can get expensive if you miss deadlines that carry penalties for missed delivery dates. However, not all late deliveries result in problems. If you plug in arbitrary dates on your purchase orders you have no way of knowing, unless someone complains, whether a late date had any effect on your production schedule. Chapter 6 discussed bringing consistency to your requested delivery dates. As part of the monitoring process you will be able to assess not only your suppliers' performance but your own performance in defining and communicating actual delivery date requirements.

Failure to Respond to Requests for Corrective Action

There are no organizations that never have problems. As a customer, you should be most concerned about their ability to respond effectively and consistently when things go wrong. The level of excellence that they bring to the problem-solving process is an excellent indicator of the health of their entire quality management system. So if a supplier responds to your request for corrective action in a timely manner and if it endeavors to uncover the cause of the problem and develop a plan to prevent recurrence, it should get credit for its work. Consider the fact that you will have already included a report of the nonconformance in your database. Now, if you have a separate category, you can look at those suppliers that took accountability for the situation and those that chose to ignore you.

Nonresponse to Queries and Requests for Technical Support

Depending on the nature of your business, the ability to reach key personnel at your supplier's location can be critical to you. Questions could relate to product information, aftermarket support, request for a quote, need to reschedule an order or to revise a specification, and so forth. The degree to which you will find it appropriate to monitor this performance indicator depends on several factors, including the type of business, your relationship with your suppliers, and the method you generally use to communicate with them.

Nonfulfillment of Additional Quality Requirements

These are quality requirements relating to certificates, reports, labeling, traceability, packaging, and so forth. Like the previous performance indicator, this one depends on the nature of your business. It demonstrates the importance of ensuring that you spend appropriate time deliberating over the criteria you will use to determine which performance indicators are most relevant to your organization.

ANALYZING AND RATING

Analysis can be as straightforward or as complex as you deem appropriate. If you're monitoring only defects and on-time delivery, you can set up a basic spreadsheet, enter the data, and create simple graphics to assess supplier performance.

If you have very few critical suppliers (I recently did an audit of a company that had only five vendors that warranted any kind of monitoring), then you may not even need a spreadsheet. You could just review records and generate a report that's discussed with managers to decide what action, if any, is appropriate.

If you have lots of suppliers and multiple indicators, you may want to establish a numerical rating system. For example, you could start every company off with 95 points. Then you subtract or add points as follows for each incident. (See figure 8.4.)

Companies get the most demerits for bad product. However, if they take the initiative to respond constructively with meaningful corrective action, they get to win back two points. They can also earn extra points by helping you out if you need something sooner than you had originally requested.

Figure 8.4 Numerical Rating System for Monitoring Vendors	
Nonconforming product	-3
Late delivery	-1
Nonresponse or late response to queries and so forth	-1/2
Nonresponse to request for corrective action	-2
Nonfulfillment of other quality requirements	-1
Acceptable response to corrective action	+2
Expedited early delivery	+1

You can establish levels that will help you to more quickly analyze the data that will be amassed. You might set up a system that assigns values based on ranges:

- 95–100: Excellent
- 90–95: Good
- 85–90: Caution; needs additional monitoring
- Below 85: On probation

Disqualifying

The outcome of your monitoring may at times lead you to the conclusion that a supplier must be disqualified or put on some kind of probation. Again, criticality is the driver.

Few transgressions are so egregious that a supplier is terminated without some notification or chance to make amends. Fraud is at the top of the list, along with other cases of malfeasance. The second would be that they have simply gone out of business (auditors do find approved vendor lists with defunct organizations still listed) or that they are rapidly becoming insolvent and unable to guarantee their continued ability to serve you. The third would be the possibility, based upon a single occurrence, that they might repeat an error that engenders risk of bodily harm. All three situations are rare but not unprecedented.

Criteria for Disqualification

What follows are possible decisions that you might make if you decide to disqualify a supplier—or to take alternate action. It's important that you define your criteria and when each of the following actions might be appropriate. You may make your decision based solely on a scoring method, or you may choose to use some other sources of information such as a reaudit, report from an on-site visit, assessment of corrective action responses, and so forth.

Disqualification versus probation

Will suppliers simply be disqualified or will they be allowed a probationary period to rectify their status? How will they be notified? Will you make them aware of your scoring system before placing an order or initiating a contract?

Revocation of dock-to-stock status

Rather than disqualifying them, you may choose to revoke their dock-to-stock status or other privileges. You may keep them as qualified suppliers but not "preferred" suppliers, meaning that you will probably choose their competitors more frequently when the opportunity presents itself.

Should you disqualify a supplier or change its status, ensure that you have a reliable method for communicating this change to key personnel in your organization. How will you make sure that someone else in your company doesn't buy from the supplier if you've taken it off the approved vendor list? This is when consideration of those individuals who aren't in the purchasing department becomes important. Think of how much time is wasted if engineering spends weeks on a design premised on a component that is available only from a supplier that you have disqualified.

Requalification and Reinstatement

It's also important to decide which methods you'll use to requalify suppliers and how you'll communicate that they have been reinstated. The methods that you use could involve abbreviated or identical tools that you used for original qualification. This will include such things as reaudit, resubmission of sample parts, improved performance indicators, or evidence of recertification to required standards.

Bringing consistency to the monitoring process will ensure that it's a value-added activity that improves your supply chain. Because these are vital partnerships for you and your suppliers, it's critical that you communicate with them and keep them informed of your requirements, your expectations, and your perception of their performance. Striving for solutions that benefit both parties sustains the health of both entities.

Chapter 9

Supplier
Corrective Actions

P art of the problem with corrective actions has long been the proliferation of requests for things that just don't meet the criteria. Significant progress has been made in recent years toward selecting problems that warrant corrective action. This has improved both the image of corrective actions and effectiveness of the results. Many folks have gone from viewing corrective actions as meaningless paper shuffles to recognizing them as sources of improvement.

Just as you need to be more judicious in your internal deliberations when launching a corrective action request (CAR), you must have defined criteria when requesting similar action from your suppliers.

It's appropriate for organizations to have a defined process for supplier corrective actions. As with other processes, it's important to look at authorizations, criteria, required documentation, sequence of activities, output requirements, verification of implementation and effectiveness, records, and closeout.

AUTHORIZATION AND RESPONSIBILITY

Who in your organization is authorized to issue a request for corrective action to your suppliers? The people who have the responsibility and the authority should understand the process, use established criteria, and work within defined guidelines. Employees in the purchasing department are the most suitable choice because they communicate regularly with the supplier's contact person. If someone else in your organization usually buys the product or service, you should solicit that individual's input in deciding if and to whom the request for corrective action should be addressed. Sending the supplier CAR (also referred to as a SCAR) to the wrong person or department almost guarantees that you won't get a response, or that the action taken won't be appropriate to the problem. If you have conducted a supplier prequalification assessment, this information may have been provided already—one of the many small benefits of audits.

The other advantage of addressing the supplier CAR to the right person is that you avoid ruffling feathers or damaging a well-established relationship. It's never a good idea to send out a CAR to suppliers without communicating with the individuals who generated the original purchase orders or the people who have day-to-day contact with them.

Criteria

You should apply the same criteria when requesting corrective action from your suppliers as you do internally.

Before you even begin to consider sending a CAR to your vendor, do your homework. Make sure that your purchase order or contract clearly and completely spells out your requirement. Check that you've provided the supplier with current, correct, and unambiguous specifications. Verify that you've communicated any engineering changes. Once you've established that the cause of the problem doesn't reside within your own walls, you can begin the process of deciding if a corrective action request is warranted.

Many people are unclear about what occurrences warrant corrective action. You must heed the important stipulation from ISO 9001, subclause 8.5.2: "Corrective actions shall be appropriate to the effects of the nonconformities encountered."

If an organization doesn't adequately define and control the input into the decision-making process, it can inundate itself—and its suppliers—with noncritical problems or anomalies better resolved through containment, remediation, or simple correction. The organization also ends up issuing the same kind of CARs to its suppliers, perpetuating valueless activities to address glitches and oversights that carry no perceptible risk to the organization or its customers.

You must have criteria for deciding when to send your supplier a CAR. If you don't establish criteria, you have no way of answering the question, "How serious is this?" The second question is, "Do we really want our supplier to expend time and money working on this problem?" Maybe you're just causing the supplier to spin its wheels on a trivial issue when it could be focusing its resources on improving processes or getting you good product on time. The proliferation of unwarranted corrective actions is counterproductive to the relationship you've built with the vendor.

By establishing criteria, you make the decision less capricious by removing the guesswork and the "gut" reactions that aren't grounded in verifiable fact. This helps to avoid presumptuous conclusions and diminishes the likelihood that one person will exercise undue influence over the decision to issue a corrective action to a supplier.

The decision is based on objective evidence that's derived from the analysis of monitoring data. It's tempered by an evaluation of risk.

Data that will be indispensable to this decision-making process will include metrics relating to such questions as:

- Has the supplier sent you defective material before?
- How many times has it missed a delivery?
- Have we notified it before of problems?
- How much is this problem costing us? (Don't forget lost production time, penalties from customers, and cost of materials to repair or rework parts.)

Combine this objective data with a risk assessment.

- Is there risk of loss of life or bodily harm?
- Will you miss an important delivery?
- Will you lose a customer?
- Will you incur a fine?
- Does this defect make you vulnerable to liability?
- Is the cost of not addressing this problem too great?

Establish a deliberation process for deciding when to issue supplier CARs. And don't ask the supplier to conduct the meaningless exercises your customers sometimes foist upon you. Corrective actions should ultimately present an opportunity to strengthen your relationship with a vendor and to improve both of your organizations.

Documentation

Once you've exercised the option to issue a supplier CAR, what documentation must be assembled? What exactly are you going to send? Be consistent. If you have several individuals who are authorized to send out CARs, make sure they know the process and have access to the required documents.

At a minimum you should send the following:

- *Corrective action request.* If you have a special form—a SCAR—check that all the information is filled out properly. If it's handwritten, make sure it's legible.
- *A cover letter.* An accompanying letter allows you to personalize your request, explain your process, define what you require from the supplier as a response, and it also gives you a chance to say thank you in advance.
- *Supporting documentation and evidence.* Include (as appropriate) a copy of the original specification, the original purchase order, inspection reports, data on previous occurrences, and a copy of the complaint from your customer. Give the supplier as much information as you possibly can so it can address the cause of this problem effectively. The assumption is that you want it to develop an action plan to prevent recurrence because this is important to you.
- *Sequence of activities.* This is a simple matter of explaining your process. You could include a copy of your procedure or work instruction. This allows the supplier to see what actions you took before you decided to request the corrective action. It serves to reinforce the fact that you didn't issue this request willy-nilly—without having done adequate research. Your supplier also has a clearer picture of:
  - ☐ Who does what
  - ☐ What has happened before the request
  - ☐ What actions will ensue after it responds.

The description could be as uncomplicated as the following example.

1. The material review board (MRB) evaluates the defective product from the vendor.
2. Various departments, as appropriate, are asked for input.
3. The purchasing department meanwhile verifies that the purchase order actually does have complete and clear specifications with no recent revisions or unauthorized changes.

4. The purchasing manager (or quality assurance manager in some organizations) checks for prior occurrence or similar problems.

5. The purchasing manager and the quality assurance manager decide jointly that a SCAR needs to be issued.

6. They assemble the requisite paperwork and the purchasing manager sends the request to the vendor.

If this is your defined process, you shouldn't deviate from it. In your process, you've decided that the purchasing manager is the person who sends the request to the vendor. Therefore, it would be inappropriate for the request to come from the vice president of sales.

Output

What do you want from the vendor? (This isn't a trick question.) If you want the vendor's response to have value for your organization, you must be specific about what you want, when, and if it should come in any particular format. What follows is a general list of things you must consider and communicate to your supplier.

■ Do you want the supplier to assign one specific person who will be your primary contact for the corrective action process?

■ Do you have a preliminary date by which you need the supplier to send you its root cause analysis, a draft of a corrective action plan, and anticipated date of completion?

■ Have you considered asking if you can participate in the corrective action?

■ Is it all right for the supplier to use its own forms, or does it have to use yours?

■ Have you put future orders on hold pending the receipt of an action plan? Are you sure the supplier knows that?

■ Do you wish to be apprised of progress if the plan is going to take several months?

■ Will you require the supplier to submit its plan for your approval?

■ What does it have to furnish in terms of inspection and/or test data or other documents before you can close it out?

Verification

How will you know what the outcome of the supplier's plan was? The same rules that apply to your internal CAR process apply to supplier corrective actions. Two forms of verification are necessary for any corrective action.

The first verification relates to implementation. How are you going to know if the supplier did what it said it was going to do? It's not that uncommon for people to put together a great plan with every intention of carrying it out. It's only later they discover that the required funds weren't available or that another individual with more authority decided to cancel the plan. What method will you employ to assure yourself that the supplier has implemented the plan it sent you? Have you decided what evidence you'll require from it or if you'll need to conduct an audit to assess the situation objectively for yourself?

The second verification relates to effectiveness. How will you—and the supplier—know that the plan worked? What statistical evidence will you require the supplier to produce? Or, again, will you want to conduct a follow-up audit?

If it's important enough to ask the supplier to expend the resources to conduct corrective action, it's worth taking the time to find out if what the supplier did worked.

Closeout

What signifies to you that everything is done? Have all the deliverables been met? Has the plan been carried out? Did it work? Are you satisfied with the outcome? Do you have all the documentation, evidence, sign-offs, and so forth that your process requires? Only when your requirements have been fulfilled is it appropriate to close out any corrective action.

Records

Who keeps the records of supplier corrective actions? The two typical choices are purchasing or quality assurance. Decide where the records will be kept, and ensure that you include them in your documentation on record retention so that key people can have access to them when needed. As with all other quality records, these are valuable assets that provide data relating to the performance of one of your key processes—supplier management.

One of the biggest benefits of supplier corrective action, besides actually solving a problem, is that it provides you with evidence of the suppliers that have been responsive, aggressive, and thorough in addressing nonconformances. This should be factored into your analysis of their performance. Vendors should get the opportunity to be recognized for their willingness to accept accountability for their errors and for expending the resources to make sure they don't happen again.

The perfect organization doesn't exist. When problems do arise, the best suppliers will be the ones that have a robust and effective process for addressing them. This is why you need to ensure that your supplier corrective action process isn't haphazard but well defined and controlled.

Chapter 10

Management Review

The placement of key features of the supply chain management process throughout various sections of ISO 9001 underscores the growing awareness of its importance. This is important when discussing management review because it highlights the role suppliers play all through the quality management system (QMS). Because the purpose of management review is to assess the status of the entire system, it follows that the review should include an analysis of supplier performance and a discussion of relevant concerns that have arisen.

Before continuing, it's appropriate to look at the ISO 9001 references and discuss their relevance and importance.

4.1 When an organization chooses to outsource any process that affects product conformity with requirements, the organization shall ensure control over such processes. Control of such outsourced processes shall be identified within the quality management system.

This requirement was discussed in chapter 3. The standard requires the organization to exercise appropriate control over outsourced processes. One reason this requirement is relevant to the management review process is the language found in the subclause below:

5.4.2 Top management shall ensure that (a) the planning of the quality management system is carried out in order to meet the requirements given in 4.1, as well as the quality objectives...

Two important concepts are presented here. The first is that top management is responsible for ensuring that the QMS is planned and carried out as described in clause 4.1. Consequently, management is also responsible for ensuring the inclusion of outsourced processes.

The other concept relates to objectives. Objectives are measurable articulations of goals. These are used to assess the effectiveness of the QMS and the achievement of organizational success.

It's appropriate to have objectives related to suppliers. As with other activities, an application of criteria will help determine which objectives are most indicative of the effectiveness of the process. Typical objectives for supplier management processes might include:

- Improve on-time delivery from suppliers to 100 percent
- Decrease supplier errors to 0 percent
- Decrease supplier base by 25 percent
- Increase number of dock-to-stock vendors by 20 percent

In each case, the objective requires action on the part of the process owner to effect an improvement in the current status of the objective. It may also require authorization by top management or the allocation of resources. Taking them in order, we can see that:

- Improving delivery may require more time for expediting or investigating and evaluating better suppliers. It may involve getting permission from management to sever a relationship with a long-standing supplier that hasn't kept pace with technology and is no longer able to deliver.
- Getting fewer errors from suppliers, especially those that are either a sole-source or a customer-mandated vendor, can be daunting because the threat of taking your business elsewhere isn't a viable option. In those instances, the most productive tack might be for top management to authorize extra money in the budget for travel so that individuals in purchasing or other process owners can visit the suppliers and work more closely with them. Alternately, management might have to put more money in the budget to correct the suppliers' (sometimes inevitable) defects.
- Decreasing the pool of suppliers has many advantages. It may not be appropriate, desirable, or necessary for some companies. For others, the monitoring and on-site audits might be so laborious and time-consuming that it would make more sense to forge stronger relations with a qualified cadre of suppliers.

5.6.2 The input to management review shall include information on ... c) process performance and product conformity.

The information that would be relevant for this requirement would include the data you've amassed and analyzed on how your suppliers are performing because this is the most accurate measure of the effectiveness of your supplier management processes. Again, depending on criticality, additional input may be appropriate if you're outsourcing significant processes. The higher the risk, the more important it is for management to be kept in the loop.

Finally, if you happen to be a distributor or wholesaler, your product conformity is almost synonymous with the conformity of products received from your suppliers: What you bring in is what you ship out. This would be different only in those instances in which you're performing extensive value-adding activities or repackaging before you send the product to your customers.

7.3.3 Design and development outputs shall... b) provide appropriate information for purchasing.

It's not uncommon for management meetings to include discussion about ongoing design projects. As part of the review, it would be appropriate to address any problems that have arisen in terms of finding and qualifying suppliers who can deliver needed materials or services to ensure that you can meet the projected release date for the introduction of your "next big thing."

If a failure modes and effects analysis (FMEA) is conducted as a step in the design process, it will also provide the organization an opportunity to assess and mitigate the risk associated with using a particular vendor. Because supplier performance is already on the management review agenda, this forum presents an optimum opportunity to digest the information presented and to determine if new evidence alters or confirms the selection of one or more key suppliers.

7.4.1 The type and extent of control applied to the supplier and the purchased product shall be dependent upon the effect of the purchased product on subsequent product realization or the final product.

The organization shall evaluate and select suppliers based on their ability to supply product in accordance with the organization's requirements. Criteria for selection, evaluation and re-evaluation shall be established. Records of the results of evaluations and any necessary actions arising from the evaluation shall be maintained.

This is the subclause that clearly defines the requirements specific to supplier selection, qualification, reevaluation, and monitoring. It's this set of requirements in the ISO 9001 standard that creates the justification for including supplier management activities in the management review because the standard recognizes them as indispensable components of the QMS.

7.4.3 The organization shall establish and implement the inspection or other activities necessary for ensuring that purchased product meets specified purchase requirements.

Again, management can assess the risk of activities such as inspection and determine what action to take based on available resources. If it decides to initiate "dock-to-stock" protocols (i.e., in which material goes directly from the receiving area to the warehouse or production floor without any incoming inspection), it's important for the decision makers to have a clear picture of what could potentially go wrong if this step were omitted from the supply process chain. It's probably easiest to assess that risk by looking at an analysis of a supplier's previous performance or by performing on-site audits.

This brings us to the last relevant requirement, upon which hangs all the information to effectively implement the preceding list of requirements: analysis of data.

8.4 The organization shall determine, collect and analyze appropriate data to demonstrate the suitability and effectiveness of the quality management system and to evaluate where continual improvement of the effectiveness of the quality management system can be made. This shall include data generated as a result of monitoring and measurement and from other relevant sources.

The analysis of data shall provide information relating to... d) suppliers.

Nowhere in this clause is it suggested that analysis of supplier effectiveness is optional. The standard very clearly says "shall"—several times.

This is the big "check" in the plan-do-check-act (PDCA) cycle. Without this step it's impossible to get to "act," which completes the cycle and initiates the next PDCA cycle. The "act" occurs during management review; management makes decisions based on presented facts and allocates resources to bring about the action plans that ensue from the decisions.

This clause also provides the best manifestation of the seventh quality management principle: a factual approach to decision making. Very briefly, ISO 9004, Section 4.3 g) states: "Effective decisions are based on the analysis of data and information."

Many of your suppliers have long-term relationships with your organization. Friendships, partnerships, and joint projects are all positive, desirable, and actual by-products of conducting business. Respect, integrity, and intuition have an appropriate role to play in the decisions that come out of these kinds of relationships. However, it's important to temper those decisions with objective evidence and distilled data.

Chapter 7 describes a monitoring example with multiple factors calculated into a rating system. It can be used as is or in conjunction with other data to present a complete picture of supplier performance. Sometimes, to make the data most meaningful to management, it's appropriate to describe the relationship between the results found in different records.

For example, a brief report on an audit visit to a major supplier can be evaluated in relation to objective performance data. Or it might be discovered that vendor self-assessments aren't providing an accurate indication of supplier capabilities. Again, the objective data can be juxtaposed to determine what follow-up action would be appropriate.

So, to sum up:

- Executive management is responsible for ensuring the establishment of processes for fulfilling goals and objectives, one of which, obviously, is supplier management.

- It's appropriate to establish objectives for supplier-related processes.

- Supplier performance is an important input into management review.

- There are times when it's important (in fact, critical) to evaluate suppliers as an input into design and development processes.

- Supplier evaluation and monitoring is a requirement—not an option.

- Sometimes receiving activities are directly related to contractual arrangements made with suppliers based upon their demonstrated ability to fulfill the requirements.

- Analysis of data relating to suppliers is an indispensable input into the management review process and a significant indicator of the effectiveness of supplier management activities.

Appendices

Appendix A   Nonstandard Supplier and Product Worksheet

Supplier	Product/service	Department/ individual authorized to purchase	Criticality (5=most critical)	Customer required?	Comments

Appendix B — Supplier Qualification and Monitoring Matrix

Supplier	Category	Criticality (5=most critical)	Qualify/ monitoring code		Customer requirement?	Comments
			Initial	Ongoing		

| Appendix C | Vendor Self-Assessment Survey |

| Company | Date_____/_____/_____ |

| Address |

| Phone | E-mail |

| Fax | Web site |

President

Quality manager

Production manager

Please furnish the following information:

1. ISO 9001-certified? (Please furnish copy of certificate.)

2. If not ISO 9001-certified, do you comply with ISO 9001 or any other recognized quality standard? (Specify.)

3. Summary of facilities and capacity. Include information relative to size of manufacturing area, number of employees, equipment technology.

4. Product(s) or service(s) supplied. Include brochure, catalog, or promotional literature.

5. Ability to furnish certifications or traceability of products or services supplied?

6. Average lead time for standard products

(continues)

Do you:	Comments:
☐ Have a quality manual? (Specify last revision date.)	
☐ Maintain a document control system?	
☐ Have controlled procedures for relevant functions? (List major functions defined in procedures.)	
☐ Have a process for maintaining customer documents and specifications?	
☐ Perform incoming inspection?	
☐ Perform final inspections?	
☐ Segregate and identify nonconforming material?	

Do you:	Comments:
☐ Have a calibration system?	
☐ Have an approved vendor list?	
☐ Have a preventive maintenance program for production equipment?	
☐ Conduct internal audits?	
☐ Have a process for addressing corrective action requests?	

(continues)

Additional comments or information

Authorized signature: _____ Date:_____/_____/_____

To be filled out by purchasing supervisor or quality assurance manager.

☐ Approved   ☐ Conditionally approved   ☐ Not approved

Comments:

Signature: _____ Date:_____/_____/_____

Appendix D — Supplier Audit Checklist

Company		Auditor(s)	Date of audit
Address		ISO Certificate?	/ /
			If yes, scope?
Phone	E-mail	Products	
Fax	Web site		
President		Purpose of audit	
Quality manager		☐ Prequalification ☐ Qualification ☐ Periodic visit ☐ Requalification	
Production manager			

(continues)

Description	Documentation used Procedure, work instructions, other documents	What are you trying to verify? What kind of evidence will you look for?	Comments and evidence Evidence or other objective means to determine level of compliance to requirements (When an item of activity is not applicable to the organization being audited, please make note in this area or mark "N/A.")
Management responsibility			
Quality policy? Mission statement? Objectives?		Does it have a mission statement or quality policy, indicating the company's commitment? Does it have published goals, objectives, targets, projections that are communicated to everyone in the company?	
Organizational chart?		Does it have an organizational chart or other document that defines responsibility, chain of command, direct reports, who does what?	
Review of quality system Quality system Quality manual		In the absence of an ISO 9001-based system, is there evidence of strategic planning, risk management, analysis of resources, problem solving, and so forth? What is management's level of awareness of the status of various processes?	

Description	Documentation used	What are you verifying?	Comments and evidence
Quality system			
Quality manual		Does it have a quality manual, and what does it include?	
Control of data and documentation			
Documented procedures and processes		What kind of documents, work instructions, SOPs, manuals, and guidance documents has the supplier developed for its processes? (Assess their adequacy.)	
Approval, access, legibility		Are the procedures and so forth that it is using approved? Do they appear to be current? Any obsolete documents? More than one revision being used? Accessible? Legible?	

(continues)

Description	Documentation used	What are you verifying?	Comments and evidence
Control of revisions and customer specifications		How does it control customer drawings and specifications (including packaging, delivery, and any other specs)? How does it handle design and engineering changes, revisions, and deviations?	
Electronic documentation		How much data are held electronically? How are the data protected? Password access? Is the system backed up? Is all information that must be protected included in the backup process?	
Records		As you go through each area or process, assess the adequacy, accessibility, and general condition of quality records. Consider: ■ Receiving ■ Inspection and test ■ Certificates of analysis ■ Certificates of calibration ■ Completed routers ■ Training ■ Corrective actions ■ Status of nonconforming material ■ Contracts/purchase orders	

Description	Documentation used	What are you verifying?	Comments and evidence
Resource requirements			
Equipment		Can the supplier tell you its production capacity? Does it have adequate machinery? Does it have redundancy (i.e., more than one machine that does the same thing)?	
Preventive maintenance		Does it have a maintenance program? What kind of records does it keep of equipment performance?	
Personnel		Adequate number of individuals qualified on each machine, function, or task (including customer service)? Method of qualification?	
Training		What kind of training? Cross training? Any industry or regulatory-mandated training? Certificates of off-site training?	

(continues)

Description	Documentation used	What are you verifying?	Comments and evidence
Purchasing			
Subcontractor evaluation documents and records		How does it evaluate suppliers? Does it conduct audits? Does it subcontract any processes? Does it track performance?	
Approved vendor list		Does it have a list? Are service providers, such as calibration houses, test labs, and so forth, on the list? When was the list last updated?	
Purchase order information		What kind of information does it require on purchase orders? How are POs generated?	

Description	Documentation used	What are you verifying?	Comments and evidence
Customer orders			
Quoting process		Verbal quotes? Records of quotes? Authority to sign quotes? Policy in case of revisions or changes (requote)?	
Verification of requirements		How does it check to make sure that it has all the information it needs to process an order and that it matches what was quoted?	
Processing of orders Adding to production		Electronically? Given to one person who enters them? Authority and responsibility? How are orders handed off to production—or shipping?	

(continues)

Description	Documentation used	What are you verifying?	Comments and evidence
Handling and communication of special requirements		Consider packaging, labeling, serializing, handling, shipping, and so forth.	
Customer approval First-piece acceptance		Does it have a mechanism for conducting first-piece inspections and getting customer approval?	
Handling or changes to orders		Quantity, delivery, cancellations, and so forth?	

Description	Documentation used	What are you verifying?	Comments and evidence
Inventory and storage			
		How are inventory data kept? How is raw material identified? Lot traceability? How are finished goods identified? General condition of warehouse?	
Inspection			
Incoming		What are the criteria for acceptance of raw materials, components, materials? How is verification recorded? Sampling plans used?	
Process control			
Define production sequence		Does it use routers? Travelers? What defines the sequence of operations?	
Production schedule		What drives the production schedule? Who controls the schedule? How well can it respond to an emergency or rush order?	

(continues)

Description	Documentation used	What are you verifying?	Comments and evidence
Verification of individual processes (identify each, including test, inspection, acceptance methods)		In this section, select manufacturing (i.e., product realization) processes and assess their adequacy and how they're controlled. Include verification/product-acceptance processes for each, as applicable.	
(1)			
(2)			
(3)			
(4)			

Description	Documentation used	What are you verifying?	Comments and evidence
Final inspection			
		What are the criteria for final product acceptance? What is the mechanism for releasing the product for shipment?	
Shipping			
		How well controlled is the shipping process? Packaging, protection of product? Company fleet of trucks or common carriers? Certificates that accompany shipments?	
Control of nonconforming product			
Segregation		Does it segregate nonconforming product?	

(continues)

Description	Documentation used	What are you verifying?	Comments and evidence
Identification		Is it properly labeled or marked to ensure against unintended use? How?	
Disposition		Does the supplier record what it does with the material?	
Measuring and test equipment			
Calibration schedule		Does it have a schedule for calibration? Are process equipment gages (such as pressure gages) on the schedule? Is there any test software? Are there test jigs that need to be periodically assessed for wear?	

Description	Documentation used	What are you verifying?	Comments and evidence
Calibration stickers (or alternative method)		How are calibrated instruments identified? Can production people distinguish between reference tools and calibrated ones?	
Records and certificates		Are certificates of calibration available? Do they identify the standard used for the verification? Do they have traceability?	
Procedure for calibration		If the supplier does in-house calibrations, does it have documented instructions?	

(continues)

Description	Documentation used	What are you verifying?	Comments and evidence
Preventive action			
FMEAs		Does it conduct FMEAs (failure modes and effects analysis)?	
Risk management		How does it assess risk and the potential for problems? What contingency plans does it have?	
Corrective action			
Customer complaints		Are formal corrective actions used to address customer complaints?	

Description	Documentation used	What are you verifying?	Comments and evidence
Root cause analysis		Is it investigating the root cause of problems?	
Corrective action plans		Is it defining and carrying out an action plan for corrective action?	
Follow-up		Is it verifying results of CARs?	

(continues)

Description	Documentation used	What are you verifying?	Comments and evidence
Internal auditing			
Audit program		Does it have an internal auditing program?	
Schedule		Is it conducting internal audits at defined frequencies?	
Trained auditors		Are the auditors trained?	

Description	Documentation used	What are you verifying?	Comments and evidence
Audit records		What kind of records does it have of audits? How are the records used? (Trace back to management. . . .)	
Analysis of data and statistical techniques			
What data analyzed		Is it analyzing/measuring any processes or features?	
Data collection		Does it use SPC? What other methods does it use to track data?	

Index

supplier monitoring 87–97; numerical rating system for 95; *see also* monitoring

supplier qualification 11, 43–57; and monitoring matrix 56, 91, 115; program for 5; *see also* qualification

supply chain 3–4, 6

T

technical support, nonresponse to 94

third-party validation 26

to-specification versus off-the-shelf 38

training 27

traveler 22

trigger 8

V

validation, third-party 26; *see also* audit

vendor self-assessment 44–50, 57, 87, 90; survey 46–50, 116

verification, of supplier corrective action 104

V

wholesalers 36; *see also* distributors